Learn the Manners of the Student of Knowledge Before you learn the Knowledge

Omer Sulayman

Table of Contents

Introduction:

Of the numerous blessings of Allah, Knowledge is one of the greatest blessings. To whomsoever Allah, the Lord of the worlds, grants the knowledge of religion, it is a sign that Allah has willed good for him.

The Prophet of Allah, peace be upon him, said:

To whom Allah wills good, He grants the understanding of religion.

This is the blessing that Allah bestowed upon the Prophets. And this is the same blessing that elevates them in rank above others. Allah gives the knowledge of revelation to His Prophets and Messengers. And through this knowledge they guide the people. They bring them out of darkness into light. This is the knowledge through which a person recognizes his Creator and Master. This is the knowledge through which one knows the straight path of Allah. This is the knowledge through which man distinguishes between Halal and Haram and between good and evil. If a person does not have this knowledge then he is blind despite having all other tools.

For there are two types of light: One is the external light that man receives from outside. And the other light is that which is in man's eyes.

If a man is blind, he cannot see despite the presence of light.

But even if a man has sight, he is not able to see when he is in darkness.

Therefore, even if he has eyes, he is unable to see.

Because of darkness, he is unable to see anything.

In the same way, no matter how intelligent a person is in the world. No matter how capable he is, no matter how much consciousness he has. If he does not have the knowledge that comes from Allah, he will continue to wander in darkness despite having a mind and understanding.

It is therefore necessary for a person to have knowledge of Allah, which is the knowledge of the Qur'an and Sunnah.

And the person who has knowledge cannot be the same as the one who has no knowledge.

The one who has knowledge follows the straight path based on evidence.

The one who has no knowledge always needs others. He cannot make decisions on his own.

Similarly, the one who has knowledge can guide others.

But the one who has no knowledge cannot guide others.

Nor can he guide himself in matters of worship or morals.

Similarly, both are not equal in terms of responsibility.

Knowledgeable people have more responsibility and confidence and their virtue is also greater than others in this matter.

By guiding others, they also earn a share of their worship and good deeds.

This is something that cannot be achieved by one who has no knowledge. Because he cannot guide others

Rather, he walks under the guidance of others. In this sense, he earns his reward but is deprived of the rewards he could earn when he guides others.

Allah, Exalted is He, says in the Noble Qur'an:

Say (O Prophet) Are those who know equal to those who do not know?

Allah revealed in this verse

That those who have no knowledge cannot compete with those who have knowledge. Why? Because the position of those who have knowledge is higher than that of others.

Allah gives them a higher position because of their knowledge and their efforts in guiding others.

A person who has knowledge and knows the Names of Allah and His attributes realizes the greatness of Allah. Such a person is not equal to the one who does not know much about Allah or the one who does not know Allah's attributes.

Therefore, knowledge from the perspective of faith is a foundation through which one's knowledge is strengthened, and through which a person's faith is strengthened.

Likewise, when the knowledgeable person guides others, his reward exceeds those who act on their own under his guidance.

A man who prays his prayers will be rewarded with five prayers. But the knowledgeable one who corrects the prayers of others, and encourages them to pray, and due to his efforts if a hundred people start praying, then along with his prayers, he also receives the reward of the prayers of one hundred people.

From this point of view, that is, the point of view of the end result, the point of view of the hereafter, it greatly increases the reward of the one having knowledge.

That is why Allah, Exalted is He, says.

Only those who have understanding will pay attention.

Here it is also known that when a person makes a mistake, a person of knowledge takes the lead in fixing it compared to the rest. The ignorant person in contrast becomes stubborn when advised.

But when a wise person makes a mistake, then when he is warned, he immediately accepts this advice.

Therefore, we come to know that one needs knowledge to accept the advice.

The student of knowledge considers the advice even if it comes from someone who is not knowledgeable. He sees what is said and not the one who says it and rectifies. Such a man acquires this capacity only as a result of high morals which is acquired by knowledge.

It is those who are endowed with understanding who receive and accept the advice.

Ponder verse number 9 of the Sura Az-Zumar in which Allah mentions the virtues of the people of knowledge.

A person should therefore try to seek knowledge. But to seek knowledge is not something that is optional, rather seeking knowledge is obligatory for every Muslim

While there is virtue in seeking knowledge, there is also an obligation.

Where Allah has called it virtuous, Allah has also declared it obligatory.

If a person does not acquire the obligatory knowledge, then he will be a sinner in the sight of Allah.

The Prophet of Allah (peace and blessings of Allah be upon him) said:

Seeking knowledge is obligatory upon every Muslim

Everything seeks forgiveness for the seeker of knowledge, even the fish in the sea.

Imam Ibn Abd al-Barr narrated it in his book Jami Bayan al-Ilrr and in Sahih Al-Jami Saghir, Shaykh Al-Albani declared it as sahih.

The number of the hadith is 3914.

It is clear from this hadith that seeking knowledge is obligatory for every Muslim, be he rich or poor, be he a man or a woman

Every responsible Muslim has to acquire knowledge, but what kind of knowledge?

Does it mean that one must acquire complete knowledge of the religion? No!

The scholars have said about this hadith, that a person who is obligated upon an action, or wants to act upon an action of worship, must acquire knowledge about it before acting.

If he wants to pray, then he must learn about prayer before he performs it.

If he wants to perform ablution, then he must learn how to perform it, how to do it according to the sunnah, and what are its rules.

So for any action that a person is responsible to do, any action that he intends to do, as long as he desires the act to be correct and to be accepted, then he must perform the act in the right way. It is obvious that this cannot happen without knowledge.

From this hadith we know, that it is obligatory for every Muslim to acquire knowledge of his religion.

The hadith that mentions the obligation of knowledge also mentions its virtues.

For a student of knowledge, everything seeks forgiveness for him. Even the fish in the sea. The question arises as to why this is so and why they pray for forgiveness for him.

Scholars say that when a student of knowledge acquires knowledge, then, as a result, he becomes a caller for good in the society. He becomes a good person and tries to call others towards good. He tries to help them to practice the religion of Allah. He tries to erase the evils of the society. He tries to bring the laws of Allah to the society. As a result of this, goodness descends from Allah. And this goodness, all people benefit from it. Even creatures benefit from it. Because of good deeds and the betterment of society, this goodness descends from Allah.

But when the society becomes corrupt, then the punishment comes from Allah because of the sinners who sin, then this loss is not only for humans and sinners, rather, it happens even to the other creations besides mankind. All creatures will then be under Allah's punishment.

So when the student erases the evils of society, then Allah's punishment does not come. And because of this, these creatures are also blessed with protection and they also benefit. Therefore, they pray for the student of knowledge, since because of him, the society improves and everyone is protected from Allah's punishment.

Hence for the student of Knowledge, everything asks for forgiveness. Even the fish in the sea do so.

So from this hadith, we come to know that the student of Knowledge will be on the path of knowledge, while he seeks knowledge. But from the very first moment of his seeking to acquire knowledge, the prayer of forgiveness for him begins with all creatures. Even the fish in the sea and the ants in their anthills pray for him. So it is a very noble thing for a man, out of part of his time to take out time to acquire knowledge of religion, that he acquires knowledge of the Qur'an and Sunnah.

Today in the 21st century, if seen in this context, then in this age and time, the importance of knowledge has increased a lot. This is because trials are also more and knowledge should be acquired to be saved from trials.

Only worship is not enough, knowledge is very important to avoid trials and tribulation, to distinguish between good and evil, and to distinguish between truth and falsehood.

It is very important for a person to acquire knowledge to avoid doubts.

We have before us a hadith of the Prophet of Allah which gives special guidance for this period.

The Messenger of Allah (peace and blessings of Allah be upon him) says:

You are in a time when, there are many jurisprudents, there are many who have deep knowledge of religion. But those who give lectures or sermons are few. There are few who ask questions, but there are many who answer. In this age. action is better than knowledge.

That is, the obligation Allah has imposed on knowledge, that is after attaining it, a person should start practicing it. Action is more necessary and better in during the time of the Prophet (peace and blessings of Allah be upon him).

The Prophet (peace and blessings of Allah be upon him) said: But soon there will come a time, when jurisprudence will decrease, those who have deep knowledge of jurisprudence and religion will remain few. In that age. there will be an increase in lecturers, speakers. There will be many who will ask questions, but there will be few who will be able to answer them. At that time, knowledge will be better than action.

This hadith tells us that in the final era, the speakers will be many, but only a few will have a deep knowledge of religion.

There will be people who respond, but those who respond correctly will be very few.

There will be fewer people who will be qualified to respond correctly.

The speakers will be many but the correct speakers will be few.

In such an age, people's questions will increase and new problems will come before the people because of technology, because of the advancement of science.

And likewise, due to being globally connected, the influential boundaries of nations will disappear in such an era.

Questions will increase a lot, new problems will arise and the need for knowledge will increase in that era.

At that time, it will be better for a person to acquire knowledge and guide people than to engage in worship.

Instead of engaging in worship, it would be better for a person to acquire knowledge and spread it.

Spread knowledge among people, guide people and answer their questions.

To bring them out of ignorance, to remove their doubts.

So this period will be like the coming era.

Rather the era in which we are living, apparently it seems to be that very era.

There are so many speakers in the present age, that it has become difficult for the listener to make a choice in this regard.

There has been an increase in those who invoke misguidance.

Those who speak evil in the name of religion have increased.

Every man has a passion for speaking, every man has a YouTube channel where he is speaking what he wants.

He speaks on such an occasion, he speaks about things he has no right to speak about.

So in such an age, it will be necessary for a person to acquire the knowledge of religion in depth.

Then, through this knowledge, to bring people out of misguidance and guide them rightly.

This hadith has been narrated by Imam At-Tabarani in Musnadush Shamiyin and

In As-Sahiha, hadith 3189, Shaykh al-Albani says that the chain is hasan.

It is known from this hadith that the importance of knowledge will increase in the last era.

This shows that the time will never come when knowledge will not be necessary but as time passes, the importance of knowledge will increase.

Therefore, a student of knowledge should not be lazy in seeking knowledge.

He should not think that, after this, he no longer needs knowledge.

Rather, he should gain much knowledge, if it is to have taqwa of Allah, to remember Allah, then such knowledge becomes a means to increase a person's faith and religion.

And it makes this person a means of good for the people.

A seeker of knowledge is learning a message not learning a course. Seeking knowledge is for the sake of Allah and not for the sake of self, not to tell people that I am better, or that I know. In seeking knowledge, it is important that it does not become your destruction leading you to kufr, disbelief. That is why it is important to know this adornment. And the most important ornament is "Laa Ilaaha Illal-Laah".

With each jewel, it's like filling your crown of honor.

We ask Allah to forgive our sins, for it deprives us of knowledge. Ameen.

Characteristics (adornments) Necessary for a Knowledge Seeker:

Either you have these characteristics or you do not, and if you have them, attribute them immediately to Allah and ask Him to keep you steadfast and not take them away from you. And if you do not have them, seek Allah's help.

1. The adornment of seeking knowledge is worship : whether you take tajweed, Arabic, fiqh, when you take Arabic it should be so that you can understand the kalaam Allah (the speech of Allah) before the kalaam of the people. You need to remember your intention that it is worship and not out of desire, like just filling your time.

The scholars said that knowledge is the "secret prayer" and a worship of the heart. Why do you learn? For Allah. It is worship, but one of the most beautiful worships. Learning, seeking knowledge is above voluntary prayer or fasting because it not only benefits you, but also society.

Knowledge is a priority; it is not a priority only if you are in the mood, because acquiring knowledge is like a struggle/effort. If your child told you that he/she is not in the mood to go to school, you would not tell him/her not to go; you would force him/her to go. How will it be for a knowledge seeker?

If Allah wills good for anyone, Allah will make him understand and comprehend religion. This is a good news from Allah. If you see that your heart is directed towards knowledge, you should thank Allah because Allah wants good for you, and it is a special provision, rizq, from Allah, and Allah chose you to acquire knowledge. Sometimes you wonder why Allah made it easy for you and not for others. You just have to say 'alhamd Allah' (praise and thanks be to Allah), and since it came to you, you need to grab it, put it in a cage, lock it up, and throw the key into the sea.

Imam Ahmad said that nothing can be equivalent to the pursuit of knowledge in relation to another voluntary worship except on the condition that the person's intention is correct. People asked how one corrects the intention. By acquiring knowledge, to eliminate ignorance of oneself and others. This means learning and teaching. There has to be input and output.

Conditions for something to be considered to be a worship:

- Ikhlas: it must be sincerely for the sake of Allah. If one does not pray or fast for the sake of Allah, then it is like an exercise. And this needs a lot of purification. When you go out to seek knowledge, what is your intention? You want to please Allah, you want Allah's praise and reward.

Surah Al Bayyinah 5:

(And they were not commanded, but to worship Allaah, and worship none but Him Alone (refraining from attributing partners to Him), and perform As-Salaat (Iqaamat-as-Salaat) and give the Zakaat: and that is the right religion).

Necessity of having four intentions:

-Intention to follow Allah's orders

-Intention to preserve religion: how? If you are writing, you are preserving knowledge, don't you know who will read it? Even if no one reads it, Allah will record it for you. You want the paper, pen and desk to witness that you are writing on the Day of Judgment.

-Intention to follow the Sunnah of the Prophet (peace and blessings of Allah be upon him): when you learn and teach you are following in the footsteps of the Prophet (peace and blessings of Allah be upon him), companions and followers.

 -Intention to defend the religion: How? If someone tries to question the religion. Solid knowledge is needed to defend religion. Where to start? With faith. If there are cracks in faith, then everything else will have cracks. He who seeks religious knowledge only to seek duniya, then he will not smell paradise.

• Following the sunnah out of love for the Prophet (peace and blessings of Allah be upon him): what makes you follow something? For love.

-Surah Al Imran 31:

Say (O Muhammad to mankind): "If you (truly) love Allaah and follow me (i.e., accept Islamic Monotheism, follow the Qur'aan and Sunnah), Allaah will love you and forgive you your sins. And Allaah is Oft-Forgiving, Most Merciful"). The scholars called this ayah, 'the ayah of trial'. If you love Allah, then you need to follow the Prophet (peace and blessings of Allah be upon him) because Allah sent him. If you love Allah and follow the Prophet (peace and blessings of Allah be upon him), Allah will love you and Allah will forgive you your sins.

-All our actions are based on love, if we do not love something, then we will not do it. A person will not taste the sweetness of faith until he loves Allah and the Prophet (peace and blessings of Allah be upon him) more than you love yourself.

-Surah Mohammed 9: That is because they hate what they Allaah has brought down (this Qur'aan and the Islamic laws, etc.), so He has made their works fruitless).

He did not say that they reject it, but they hate it. They pray but they hate it, the decree comes, but they hate it, like sickness. There must be love when you do something. Imagine asking for water and one son says 'take it' and another says 'this is for you my mother'. There is a big difference, you would end up telling the first one not to do it if that is his attitude. So the foundation of our actions needs love.

2. Adornment of being according to the way of the companions (predecessors): how they used to learn the tawheed that we should follow, or how they interpreted the Quran. Some people try to put scientific foundation to worship, for example, if you

prostrate, you will release negative energy. And this is a deviation because the intention is for the body and not to please Allah. The deviation comes through scientific reasoning or through philosophy, because it is about questioning everything, to the point that you no longer believe in anything.

The adornment of the seeker of knowledge is to fear Allah (the Most High): not fearing Allah leads to corruption and destruction.

Surah Fatir 28: It is only those who have knowledge among His servants who fear Allaah. Verily, Allaah is Almighty, Forgiving). When you know Allaah and His greatness, you will fear Allaah. You will fear that knowledge will be taken away from you. Sometimes people memorize the Qur'aan but without any application. This is learning for the sake of learning without fear of Allah. Without fear means that there is no application of knowledge and this will lead to failure and there will be no blessing in knowledge. Sometimes there is blessing in knowledge, how? There is application, you change, you are a different person. If a person is forgetting the knowledge, then you need to watch yourself, because there is no application. Sometimes you feel like you know and then you forget. Especially with ayat from the Quran, if you memorize it and then forget it, then it didn't enter the heart.

4. Constant observation/caution ornament: need to always watch your expressions, your heart, your actions. If people are afraid of being fined for speeding, they will be cautious; if they are not afraid, they will not care.

Similar to the previous point, fear will result in constant observation. The seeker of knowledge will not react badly if others react badly to him. It is their sin to react badly, so you will not want to follow their example as a seeker of knowledge. Before you say anything, you must watch your heart and your tongue.

Observation, prudence will lead to the ihsan: do not say but what is good. As if you see Allah, and if you do not see Allah, then Allah sees you.

5. Adornment of 'lowering the wings': the tree, when it is full of fruits, will be lower, when it has no fruits, then it is higher. You cannot learn and have arrogance, you need to be humble. You can't say I know this; you don't need to tell me.

They are satisfied with what they have, and have no desire for what others have.

They have tolerance and forbearance; they will not rush to the judgment and punishment of others. For example, someone comes and tells him that you did such and such a thing, and he will not say I did not do this. They are lenient, they will not say I will not talk to this person again. And this will happen to prove their truthfulness. For example, once a woman wanted to go out to seek knowledge, and every time her child falls ill. And every time it is the same, so she went to seek knowledge, and the child became well. Subhan Allah.

Don't spread your problems and negativity to others. You will only infect others. Life is according to how you see things, if you see it as 'gardens of paradise' you will see it like this. If you always complain, it's hot, it's this and that, then you will see it that way.

We do not like to be insulted by others.

Allah's Apostle said: "Allah, the Most High, said: "The son of Adam slights Me, and he should not slight Me, and he disbelieves in Me, and he should not. As for his despising Me, it is that he says that I have a son; and his disbelief in Me is his claim that I will not create him again as I created (him) before."). - Al Bukhari

6. Adornment of contentment (with the worldly) and not wanting what others have: I need to be content with all that Allah has given me and not look at others and what they have. You will be distracted if you look at what others have, where is the time then for you to spend seeking knowledge?

 People love those who don't look at what they have. And that person will be qualified to be a seeker of knowledge.

 Everything you do not possess, you end up loving it, and the moment you buy it and possess it, you no longer love it. Example: a man marries a very beautiful woman, and the moment he starts looking at others, he does not find beauty in his wife. Subhan Allah.

 Adornment of being beautified with the radiance of knowledge: what is the radiance of knowledge? It is sakina, tranquility, dignity. It knows when to speak and when to react, there is etiquette. When you know it is worship, you will do it in the best way. Presentation is important, within limits, when you are spreading the message. You have to be presentable and sit appropriately.

8. Adorn the best of character: start with a smile, the more you smile, the more you understand and the happier you are. Imagine someone frowning; it lowers your mood and the mood of the people around you. The Prophet (peace and blessings of Allah be upon him) frowned once and it is mentioned in the Quran. When you smile you are more approachable, within limits of course.

9. Gentleness ornament: Although it is included in the previous point, it has a point of its own, because it is necessary to underline it. It is necessary to be gentle, soft and polite when spreading the message. Especially when a woman is speaking to another woman, one should be even gentler.

Hadith:

Allah is Gentle and loves gentleness, and grants for it the reward that He does not grant for harshness" (Sahih)

Gentleness also includes being gentle with devices, not knocking on the door, or shouting while driving, or driving erratically.

10. Adorn yourself with observation and devote time to it: especially when speaking, think before you speak.

When speaking: Are they good words or not? Can you offend someone?

When studying: Even when you want to study, do not rush.

When asking a question: And slow down, slow down when you have a question. Be patient and ask the question at the end. When you seek knowledge, you will find that your questions will be answered at the right time because Allah will bring it to you when the time is right.

11. Adornment to be firm: when you learn something, be firm with it. For example, if you go to class, don't leave it halfway and change your course. Thank Allah and ask Him for steadfastness. Acquiring knowledge is like an ocean, there are parts we can't swim in, but ask Allah for steadfastness so you don't drown.

If someone brings you news, you have to verify it.

We ask Allah to grant us these characteristics of the seeker of knowledge and always for His pleasure. Ameen.

Knowledge seeker's ornament

Those who believe and receive knowledge are the ones who rise. Not all who seek knowledge will attain it, i.e. receive the knowledge of Allah.

Allah does not give knowledge randomly, but on the basis of knowledge and wisdom. So ask Allah to make us worthy to receive His knowledge. Ameen. We must seek knowledge for the sake of Allah in order to be elevated.

The Knowledge Seeker is a Passionate Seeker of Knowledge

Closeness and connection with knowledge : The seeker of knowledge cannot be far from knowledge, he feels that he will be lost if he moves away from it. Ibn Qayyim said this. And that he said it shows that this is what he felt.

Busy with his passion : he feels that he is blinded from other things. As if knowledge is a person, and they know that this knowledge will accompany him in his grave. Subhan Allah. The liar will be distracted from seeking knowledge.

Blamed for his passion : people will blame him for being busy with knowledge, but he doesn't care because he can taste the sweetness of knowledge. Nothing can change his feelings for seeking knowledge. The one who is not firm in seeking knowledge if blamed, will reduce or give his pursuit of seeking knowledge another thought.

The intensity of passion for knowledge is the highest : it is a more intense feeling than passion for money. Ibn Qayyim was so passionate that he found a book in the library, and he could not buy it and there were no photocopying machines, so he wrote the whole book by hand. Notice how blessed we are to have easy access to books, alhamd Allah. Sheikh Al Albani, by name he was from Albania, he was not an Arab but he was a seeker of knowledge. So it makes no difference whether he is Arab or non-Arab.

Adornment of applying beneficial knowledge :

Dua: O Allah we ask You for beneficial knowledge. Beneficial' is that which will bring good from it, and bring you closer to Allah, and bring good to society, and keep you away from evil, and make you steadfast.

(I) Signs of beneficial knowledge :

Beneficial knowledge is applied : for example, if you memorize the Qur'an, there must be application. First you must believe in it. After believing in it, there must be a reaction. You will become attached to Allah. Sometimes the shaitan will discourage us by making us think that we are not doing enough from the outside, when we should first have a movement of the heart.

If a person does not apply the knowledge, then the knowledge will not be beneficial, it will be detrimental. Or just to finish. The Quran will either be with you or against you. That is why the sirat (path) is a very thin line.

He hates it when people call him "he is good" or praise or elevate him : He hates it because he is afraid. He will not praise himself or boast. A knowledge seeker who praises himself is not a true knowledge seeker. If he does, then his knowledge will be harmful. He need not say that he has memorized the Qur'an. He will be humble.

3. Escape from fame and duniya : does not seek knowledge for position.

4. He will not say that he is an expert in knowledge : he eliminates any kind of desire. He does not want a title, but people out of respect give him a title. The scholar himself calls himself a "knowledge seeker".

 Think bad about yourself and good about others : the more you think bad about yourself, the more you become attached to Allah. You think that you are poor and miserable and that you are full of faults, so you need Allah. We do not think badly of ourselves out of discouragement, but out of attachment, because we are slaves. Do not think well of yourself. And think well of others, do not judge others. Many times after learning, a person starts to categorize people and look down on people for doing something, when they themselves were once in that situation. For example, complaining about people being dressed a certain way, when they could have been in that same situation. A bad impression, even once, can remain for a long time, even if someone always treats you well.

(II) Purification of knowledge :

Just as you need to purify your money by giving it to the poor, because it will purify your heart of diseases and bless the rest of your money. In the same way, knowledge has to be purified so that knowledge will be blessed and purify the heart.

Spread the knowledge : the best investment is to do something that helps the largest number of people and for a long time. For example, if you want to be a teacher, people want to avoid young children, but they are the best investment. For example, if you teach them Surah Al Fatiha, and you are the first to teach it to them, you will get a reward for every time they read it or if they teach it. Children will remember all the good you do to them and they will remember all the bad you do to them.

Today there are many different ways to disseminate knowledge, especially with today's technology.

You can spread knowledge by your actions. For example, you learn about Allah Al Wakil, and you apply it with your actions. You are relaxed, less stressed, and people can see it. Or you learned about patience and you show patience, so you set an example. You can purify knowledge by setting an example.

Encouraging good and forbidding evil: a means for the purification of knowledge.

When you do the purification of knowledge, you get increments, Allah will bless it and increase you in knowledge and purify your heart. People think that if I teach everything then I have nothing left. This is not true. The more you spread, the more Allah will give you. The condition is that you live under the shadow of "Laa Ilaaha Ilal-laah". Why do angels lower their wings and ants pray for the seeker of knowledge? Because it is a noble act.

Many teachers learn from students, from their reactions, their speech, their interaction, their reflections. Sometimes you find students who are mubarakin, 'blessed' for their teachers. One student can make a suggestion and it becomes a whole class. Sheikh As Saadi wrote a book based on a question from his student. Subhan Allah. The question was, what are the means to multiply rewards? Subhan Allah.

When knowledge is disseminated and taught, it becomes firmer.

(III) Adornment of honoring knowledge :

▪ It's not about being arrogant, but imagine you have knowledge and you come to a meeting. You want to show the honor of having knowledge. For example, you want to tell them about Allah. If you see that people are getting bored and are not appreciating, then you are humiliating knowledge and yourself.

▪ If you are the bearer of knowledge, don't humiliate knowledge, if you want to act upon it, make it honorable. Don't let others say, 'oh here comes this person and know that they are going to lecture us'.

(IV) Adornment of keeping the knowledge of being humiliated

▪ For example, would you give expensive jewelry to a child? No. Then how would it be for beneficial knowledge? It should be given to whom it suits. Can one speak of being blessed to someone who does not magnify Allah? Otherwise, it is humiliating knowledge.

▪ Another example, if doing a very advanced tafsir class, you cannot give it to everyone, because some people will not appreciate it.

▪ It's like giving a piece of jewelry to someone who won't appreciate it and won't take care of it.

▪ There is much reward for knowledge, but it is all a provision from Allah. Allah is preserving knowledge through those who appreciate it and are worthy of having it. Subhan Allah. May Allah make us part of those whom He chooses to preserve knowledge. Ameen.

(V) Adornment of not accepting if something is wrong but not rushing to change, but not letting it go and saying it's okay :

• If someone is doing something wrong, you will not quickly tell them that it is wrong, but in your heart you deny it. Otherwise, if you tell them it's wrong, then they will eventually leave. But you delay reprimanding them because they may change over time. On the other hand, you should not let it go completely and tell them it is OK without ever correcting them.

• If you force people to change, you generate hypocrisy in society. We must counsel them in such a way that we attract them and not repel them.

• So it must be a middle way of using wisdom to get them to reform.

Classroom manners :

Classroom presence: Proper seating, and good manners in asking a question and listening. Remember that you are doing this for Allah, not for someone else. If you don't know what to do, then it will become a fitna for people. Besides you are in the presence of the angels and Allah knows what is in your hearts. Do not be of those who are sitting with their bodies, but their hearts are elsewhere. When your heart is there, Allah will reward you.

• You could also be teaching two equal classes, but you feel motivated for one and not the other, why? Because there is a lack of presence of heart in the meeting. Subhan Allah. There has to be interaction between students and teacher with the heart present.

• Imagine that a principal enters the classroom, everyone is formal and proper. Now imagine in a study circle, where there are angels present and watching and recording everything, and the angels are there up to the 7th heaven, and Allah is witnessing everything. Subhan Allah.

• Your eagerness shows through your enthusiasm and joy, and that encourages the teacher and enhances the learning experience.

▪ Make a mistake: If a teacher makes a mistake, it does not mean that you stop attending class. When correcting, it should be done without embarrassment, if it can be done, then it should be done in private. But if a mistake is made that confuses halal with haram, or a mistake in the Qur'an, then it should be corrected immediately. Ask Allah to guide you when you decide to correct.

▪ Irritating others: Some students try to push the button by irritating the teacher.

▪ Show interaction: teacher asks if everything is understood, asks questions. Everyone benefits.

▪ If you want to drop a class: then you should tell the teacher instead of doing it behind your back to attend with another teacher for example, so that it does not cause a fitna. It is better to talk it out because the teacher can advise you if attending another class may lead to benefit or harm you.

We ask Allah to make us bearers of knowledge and to fulfill their rights for the sake of Allah and in a way that pleases Him. Ameen.

What nullifies the seeker of Knowledge

(1) Failure to apply what has been learned :

For example, memorizing the Quran but not changing the heart.

Reasons for non-application:

1. Lack of belief in Allah : the more you believe in Allah, the more you will apply yourself, it is correlated. The more you are attached, the more you will trust and the more active your heart will be. Belief in Allah is one of the pillars of faith. You believe that Allah watches you, listens to you, knows what is in your heart. And when you believe in Allah, you submit to Allah, you are sincere. When you eat, you see that Allah is Al Razaq, The Provider, The Merciful, The Loving and you feel grateful, submitted, how loving Allah is in giving us different foods with different colors. And you are honoring yourself when you are a slave of the Most Perfect, not of someone like you or below you.

If a person lacks faith in Allah, eventually his heart will harden because he has been following his desires all along. His reactions will be according to his desires, he will shout, he will scream. Whereas those who believe and know will be sure not to react incorrectly. The more you believe in Allah, the more you will safeguard yourself from sins. Before telling people don't do this or don't do that. Tell them about Allah, because people love perfection.

We ask Allah to protect us from hypocrisy, from those who pray only because others pray, or learn because others learn. Even in the grave, when asked who is your Lord? They will say we heard people say Allah, so we said. Imagine they did nothing for Allah, but only for the people.

Allah will give the greatest delight to the believers in seeing His face. Why? Because they saw Him in their hearts, and now Allah will enable them to see Him with their eyes. The greatest punishment for the disbeliever is not to see Allah. Why? Because they ignored every sign from Allah that was sent to them in this life, and they will be blinded to see Allah in the hereafter.

2. Lack of belief in the Day of Judgment : we believe in a Day of Judgment in which we will die, be taken away by angels, placed in our graves, resurrected, gathered for judgment, actions weighed in the balance, cross the sirat, settle accounts in qantara, and finally enter paradise only for the true believer.

He who does not believe in a Day of Judgment will not take his deeds and actions seriously.

3. Lack of knowledge in the virtues of the actions: when the virtues are known, then it is done from the heart. If not, then it becomes mere repetition. There are virtues in the pursuit of knowledge, in wudu, when you visit the sick, there are 70,000 angels pleading for you, you are in a garden in paradise, and Allah is there. So we have to go over the virtues.

4. He thinks he will live a long life, so he doesn't need to do it now: he adopts a very lazy approach. You may regret it later, perform good deeds another day. When you know that you can die at any time, then you want to do good deeds all the time.

3. No good example in life: what makes children feel motivated to wash, clean, pray? By your actions. When they see you do it, they will do it. Whether you are kind to others or yell, they will pick up on it.

6. Shaitan's war: the moment we are born, he has declared war on us. His mission is to take us to hellfire. That is why he will deceive us, conspire and give us bad ideas. If you don't know Shaitan's tricks, you will fall into the trap. If people do you wrong, and you are lenient, then the Shaitan will come and tell

you what happens to your dignity, honor. When you remember that the Prophet (peace and blessings of Allah be upon him) was ridiculed and beaten, and yet he forgave people, then what happens to us when we compare it to what we are going through? Or the shaitan may mislead people by saying that Islam is suitable for Arabs because of their culture, ie: women wear hijab because it is part of the culture, so a non-Arab might doubt, but Islam was sent for all mankind. And not only mankind, but even the jinn, imagine the jinn apply the same rules of Islam, then how can you say you are a different culture when it suits a completely different entity, subhan Allah.

The secret is that when you are learning beneficial knowledge is to put yourself on the spot. When you feel that with learning more knowledge you are so far behind, and as if you have so many mistakes, then this is a good sign.

(2) Daydreaming:

▪ They are not avid seekers of knowledge. They assume or claim to be knowledge seekers, but they are not.

(3) Be aware whether you are a 'one-span' knowledge seeker:

A scholar once said, going into the field of knowledge is three parts (hand spans), so the scholar said don't be one of those who are still stuck in the first span:

▪ First span: just start with knowledge and have arrogance, learn and feel proud of yourself for knowing something. Your heart can go higher. Don't get stuck in this span. If you get stuck in this span, then it negates the knowledge.

Second span: after learning more knowledge, be humble. It's true that you know and others don't, but be humble about it.

▪ Third span: the deeper you get into knowledge, the more you realize that you know nothing. And this is a good sign to reach this level. It is the opposite of seeking 'duniya' knowledge. From knowing nothing to becoming an expert. Subhan Allah.

Moses said that he was the most knowledgeable so Allah sent Al Khidr who had more knowledge. And each had a different style of knowledge, one divine and one legislative. So they said that if they combined all their knowledge, it would not be even a drop close to the knowledge of Allah. And what about us, who are we to be arrogant with our knowledge? Subhan Allah.

(4) Be aware of moving forward when you are not qualified :

▪ This can nullify knowledge. A person cannot answer fatwa questions if he does not have full knowledge because it is an amana (trust), and it can affect the person's path. There are scholars for fatwas.

▪ If a person comes forward, then it shows a disease of the heart, shows his pride, and may say things that Allah has not said, and will cause him not to accept the truth. If you have knowledge, Allah will bring the position to you. For example, the messengers did not say that they wanted to be messengers, Allah chose them to be messengers.

(5) Be aware that you are a scholar :

▪ Anyone who calls himself a scholar, then this nullifies knowledge, this is different from being called a scholar by others.

▪ Imagine someone who calls himself a hafidh, when in fact he is not. And calling yourself a scholar shows people that you are trying to get that title, that you are there to show off.

• If you are placed in this honorable position of seeking knowledge, then show gratitude to Allah.

(6) Reaction when others make a mistake :

• Never set yourself up for competition. A knowledge seeker is not happy when others make mistakes. For example, when we get test scores, we compare ourselves with others, and we feel happy that if we get better grades. Unfortunately, we have been brought up to be better than others. But we should be good for ourselves, for the sake of Allah - this is tawheed. We do not want to incorporate shirk.

• If you find an error, do not proclaim it or make it public. Approach the person and tell them privately.

• Everyone makes mistakes, don't make a person look bad in the eyes of people. You must love for yourself what you love for others.

(7) Do not fall into doubt :

• Don't make your heart like a sponge that receives all the results and observes everything. You need to be aware of sitting with those who have doubts, because you are afraid to observe and pick up on their doubts.

▪ For example, those who debate how Allah rose above the throne? We should limit ourselves to believe, but do not go deep because it may spoil your faith. Many times when listening to debates, the speaker who raises doubts is good at talking, so don't listen and avoid him.

▪ Ibn Taymiyah advised his student Ibn Qayyim, do not make your heart a sponge, for if you are in the field of dawah, then you will surely hear doubts. So make your heart a crystal clear vessel without doubts.

▪ Doubts will make you see right as wrong and wrong as right, and don't spread doubts to people either.

(8) Be aware of groups and circles :

▪ You seek knowledge by Allah and Allah teaches you. And now within the same sect there are groups loyal to a certain sheikh. We have to be under the shadow of 'Laa ilaaha illal-laah'.

▪ So many heart diseases can come when there is division between one and the other.

(9) Do not expose secrets :

▪ If they tell you a secret, you cannot divulge it. For example, if someone comes to ask you about a personal marital problem, you cannot go and tell others that this person has a marital problem.

▪ If a person tells you and is shaking their head left and right, then it's a secret. Don't share it with others even if they don't tell you it's a secret.

▪ If a person tells you something that you can share as an example for others, then that's fine, but don't mention their name.

(10) Passing information to others to create problems

▪ No need to tell others that this person said such and such about you. And then go back and tell the other, this person said such and such. This causes rifts between people.

People who try to make trouble for each other, by namima (talebearing), the punishment of the grave will befall him. He will not enter paradise until he purifies himself.

▪ The Prophet (peace and blessings of Allah be upon him) said to others: do not speak to me about someone, so that when I meet them, I may have a pure heart in preaching to them.

(11) Speak harshly and badly to everyone :

▪ Do not speak badly and negatively to others. He cannot speak in vulgar and harsh language to others. A seeker of knowledge would not speak in such a manner.

▪ It does not mean that a person cannot speak in a loud voice, because some people have loud voices, but not to speak in harsh words.

(12) Excessive jokes :

▪ It doesn't mean you can't joke, you can be lighthearted, but not from the beginning to the end of the conference always joking.

▪ Even when the Prophet (peace and blessings of Allah be upon him) joked, he was telling the truth about it. Once an old woman told the Prophet (peace and blessings of Allah be upon him) to pray for her to enter jannah (Paradise). He said that old women do not enter jannah, because you enter young.

▪ If you joke a lot, then people don't know when you're being sincere or not, so they won't take you seriously.

(13) To come between two people talking :

▪ One person is talking and one person is answering, a knowledge seeker would not get between two people discussing. One person getting in the middle is just to show that they know, and there is no need to do so.

(14) Hate :

▪ For example, the story of the two sons of Adam. The brother was jealous of the other and then it turned to hatred.

▪ What good is knowledge if there is hatred? Knowledge comes to purify the heart, it defeats the purpose if the heart has hatred.

▪ Even if the person's opinion is different, it does not mean hating him or her.

(15) Jealousy :

▪ If a person is jealous, how can he be worthy of having divine knowledge? That is why one must be purified from the beginning.

▪ It is a great fitna if you compare yourself with others, seeing where they came and where you are. Some people feel jealous of each other over a car, a house, but it is more serious to feel jealous over religion.

▪ The good news is that you can detect jealousy because you can feel the pain in your heart. Then you can purify and reform yourself.

▪ Jealousy is wanting to take away a person's blessing, and is a major sin because it burns your good deeds. One can also commit fitnah by praising another person in front of another, thus provoking his jealousy. For example, a mother who praises her son and compares him to another brother can become a fitnah by putting jealousy in the heart of one of the sons.

Subhan Allah. Imagine initiating a sin. We ask Allah not to put us in the position of putting jealousy on others. Ameen.

▪ Love for others what I love for myself. Not to hate what others have.

▪ Jealousy turns the heart away from Allah, for the heart is now occupied in conspiring to take away the blessing.

(16) Thinking badly of others :

▪ This also includes suspicion, because it can lead to sin. For example, between husband and wife, they will check and spy on each other.

▪ Whoever spies, will see things that will make him think wrong ▪ Why? Because they opened this door, the shaitan will make them see things wrong.

(17) Sitting with an innovator :

▪ If you sit with an innovator, then you can make others think that it is okay, or that a knowledge seeker agrees with the innovator.

We ask Allah to make us seek beneficial knowledge only for His sake, and not to nullify it. Ameen.

- Surah Isra'a 80: (And say (O Muhammad SAW): My Lord! Let my entrance be good, and (likewise) may my exit be good. And grant me from You an authority that will help me (or a firm sign or a proof)).

- Even if you've been seeking knowledge for years, you have to go back and make the entry truthful.

Knowledge seeker's disposition - What is knowledge?

Knowledge is the opposite of ignorance.

Knowledge is to realize and know something as it really is. It is not a conjecture or a guess, that is not knowledge. Knowledge is firmness.

The knowledge we need is what Allah (the Most High) has revealed to the Prophet (peace and blessings of Allah be upon him) - which is the Qur'an and Sunnah. This is the evidence for knowledge to be firm. This is the divine knowledge that comes from the Qur'an and Sunnah.

Surah Az Zumar 9: (Say: "Are those who know equal to those who do not know?")

It is not knowledge when someone speaks without evidence, i.e. not from the Qur'an and Sunnah. We want to be among those who know.

• Ibn Al Qayyim, may Allah have mercy on him, said that there are six levels in knowledge :

1. Excellent questioning : means not asking all types of questions. There are ways to ask questions - this is the first level.

2. Excellent listening : you used to learn by asking questions, very restless, but now you learn by listening and observing.

3. Excellent understanding : the knowledge is firmly rooted, do you stop here? No. And you will see that Allah (the Most High) will open for you more, subhan Allah.

Memorization : the knowledge that you have understood - is memorized. It is not memorized from the first level.

Teaching : now you can transmit the message. Teaching is not reading from a paper, it has to be in the heart, it is memorized. And when you project it, then there will be feeling with it, it is not just reading from a paper.

6. Acting on the knowledge : the moment you talk to someone, and the other person is also willing to listen - then Allah (the Most High) opens up for both the speaker and the listener. There is barakah in groups, not in being alone. At this level the fruits of knowledge are obtained.

▪ Knowledge is a lifelong journey, it is not something you will finish. Therefore, you must take care of your supplies throughout this journey.

Knowledge Seeker Provision - What is a Knowledge Seeker?

Hadith Narrated by Abu Hurairah (may Allah be pleased with him): that the Messenger of Allah (peace and blessings of Allah be upon him) said: "Whoever takes a path to gain knowledge, Allah makes the path to Paradise easy for him"). - Jami'at-Tirmidhi 2646

This path is always open, an easy path, "green light". It also means a desire and wanting to walk that path, knowledge in this case. Why is it a desire? Because you like it. That's why you can't force anyone to learn.

Qur'anic scholars and Hadith scholars are so much into seeking knowledge day and night, they don't even want to waste time eating, so they eat things that can be easily swallowed, subhan Allah.

Alhamdullillah now everything is so accessible with the internet - we have to do a lot of shukr for this, alhamdullillah. And when we are grateful, then Allah (the Most High) will increase us. One of the worst things a seeker of knowledge can do is to criticize, where is the gratitude? Saying that the seats are uncomfortable, that it is too hot/cold, etc... subhan Allah. At least there are angels surrounding the study circles, subhan Allah. There are places where people have to sit on the floor, with no facilities to learn, so we have to be thankful. And when one person complains, it has repercussions for everyone: we don't want the blessing to be removed. If someone is teaching, it is important that they inform their students so that the blessing is not removed. We all want to be mubarakeen, it is not only up to the teacher, but also up to the students. You can notice a difference between study circles, why? It is because of the hearts - so we all want to be blessed, what is the point of having hearts full of ingratitude, hatred, jealousy, etc, subhan Allah.

This path is not easy, because there is so much fitna, 'self', desires, etc. It is not about the teacher - sometimes a teacher can be so 'good' and no one understands and a teacher can be simple but everyone understands, why? Because only Allah will make things easy. And Allah (the Most High) will make the way to paradise easy, how? He will bring you all the means of paradise, it is open, subhan Allah. Sometimes you are searching, you may not find it today or tomorrow, may be after a year - but nothing is lost with Allah. You will find that Allah (the Most High) will bring means that will make paradise closer. The more good deeds you do, the closer you will be to paradise, all the while faith increases. Allah (the Most High) will give you ikhlas, and is preparing you to be the bearer of knowledge, subhan Allah.

▪ The heart of the knowledge seeker

Why is it the "heart"? Because the vessel needs to be pure to receive knowledge. Never think that you will reform, or be a teacher, or a scholar without reforming and focusing on your heart. You may be learning, but if the heart is not pure, then that knowledge will be against you on the Day of Judgment. Knowledge without a heart is like a body without a soul, subhan Allah. Someone with little knowledge but a good heart is better than someone with a lot of knowledge but a bad heart. A bad heart can lead especially to arrogance.

The heart needs to be always purified, and while you are learning you need to check your heart. You need to feel if your heart feels arrogance, or envy, etc. before it becomes a disease.

Knowledge Seeker Provision - What is provision?

▪ Surah Al Baqarah 197: (And take a provision (with you) for the journey, but the best provision is At-Taqwa (piety, righteousness)).

Taqwa is a very broad word that means to abstain from anything that displeases Allah (the Most High) and to love, hope and fear Allah.

We need taqwa all the time, but for the seeker of knowledge it is especially necessary. What will keep you steadfast in taqwa?

Taqwa is a Provision for a Knowledge Seeker - You need to remember...

▪ Virtues of knowledge : It is easier with the help of Allah (the Most High) to protect your knowledge than to protect your money, why? Because knowledge is in your heart, no one can take it away from you, subhan Allah. Knowledge is the inheritance of the prophets and messengers - therefore it has much value.

- Need to remember the rules for the pursuit of knowledge: - it is MANDATORY for every Muslim/Muslimah. It is important to know who Allah is? How to worship Him? - It is important to know the principles of the faith. How can a person succeed then? Children need to go to school and if they don't, they will fail. However, we are not serious about seeking the fundamentals of knowledge. Will Allah (the Most High) ask you whether you have a degree or not? No. But He will ask you: "Who is your Rabb? What is your deen? Who is your Messenger? Yes, subhan Allah. These are the questions of the grave, and it is obligatory to learn this.

- Manners of the seeker of knowledge :

Those who lack manners may come to harm people. The Prophet (peace and blessings of Allah be upon him) warned us of a people who have knowledge and worship much, but have no manners.

What are the manners of a knowledge seeker ?

Seeking knowledge is worship : just as when you pray, recite the Qur'an, do dhikr or tawaf, seeking knowledge is also worship. Like any other worship, it requires devotion, concentration and focus. Seeking knowledge is not just acquiring information, but worship - your heart must be filled with love, fear and hope of Allah (the Most High). It is not that you are seeking knowledge and your heart is elsewhere. May Allah (the Most High) forgive us. Ameen. Some scholars say that knowledge is even a worship of the heart , it is a secret prayer , and it is a struggle for the sake of Allah (the Most High) because you really have to fight against yourself to seek knowledge. Sometimes you may be listening to an online lecture, and you are texting/answering the phone, etc - and it is actually said that the rights of the teacher come first, even if you can't see them, subhan Allah.

The point is that Allah (the Most High) is watching you - may Allah (the Most High) forgive us. Ameen: And how will you have this sensitivity wherever you are learning? When you know that knowledge is worship, subhan Allah. For it to be worship, you have to do it with:

Ikhlas / Sincerity : for the sake of Allah (the Most High), and seeking knowledge with sincerity will take you very high, even the angels, ants and fish will seek forgiveness for you. And seeking knowledge without sincerity, will take you very low - they are the first to enter Hellfire. May Allah (the Most High) protect us. Ameen.

Following the Sunnah

Follow the way of the righteous predecessors : what is their way? 'We listened and obeyed' - this means to give up any dispute in matters of religion. This is the opposite of arguing again and again. If you want to gain knowledge easily, then stop the disputes. You may find that deviation occurs as a result of arguing, subhan Allah. There are ayat and hadith - do not argue about it, and not even with yourself. Arguing will never bring anything good, and it is even worse with regard to religion. That is why the Prophet (peace and blessings of Allah be upon him) said to give up arguing, even if you are right. And may Allah (the Most High) protect those of us who started the argument. Ameen: What will make things difficult in religion? When people argue. We are not here to say who is right and who is wrong, who is the winner and the loser because Allah (the Most High) will judge. The way of arguing is the way of philosophers, who only teach you how to argue and this will affect your belief. So, if you are in an argument, withdraw and do not open anything from arguing.

Surah Al An'am 153: ("And verily, this is my Straight Path, follow it, and follow not (other) paths, for they will turn you away from His Way. This is what He has commanded you to become Al-Muttaqûn.)

Imam Adh Dhahabi (may Allah have mercy on him) said that there is nothing more hateful than arguing.

3. Fear of Allah (the Most High) accompanying you all the time

Surah Fatir 28: (Only those fear Allaah who have knowledge among His servants. Verily, Allaah is Almighty, Forgiving).

Who fears Allah (the Most High)? Those who have knowledge. It is a safeguard so that you don't transgress - what makes you not to argue, boast, etc.? When you know that Allah (the Most High) is watching you - then there is fear. Imagine two people seeking knowledge, one fears Allah (the Most High) and the other does not. The one who does not fear Allah (the Most High) and rather fears the people or the teacher, what will happen to him? There will be no barakah in his knowledge, he will forget knowledge. But when you fear Allah (the Most High) and know that He is watching you, then you will not forget the knowledge - Allah (the Most High) will give you success, barakah and guidance, subhan Allah.

4. Watchful of Allah (the Most High): believe and feel that Allah (the Most High) is watching you - you are under His watchfulness, and He is especially watching your heart and every movement - what you say, what you think, how you feel, etc. Imagine you are writing and someone is staring at you, watching you, you will become aware and be careful what you do - even if they are just watching your exterior. And what about Allah (the Most High) who is watching everything that goes in and out, subhan Allah.

Good manners : what you like for yourself, you should do for others. You like people to smile at you - so smile first. You like people to speak politely to you - so speak politely to others. And remember that when dealing with people, don't even wait for them to thank you.

Surah Al Insan 9: (We do not desire reward or thanks from you)

You should also be patient with people and forgive them, and also do not expect to receive good manners from them. Do not have good manners just to return them to others; for example, if someone says salam, I will say salam; if they smile, I will smile.

6. Be content with what you have (regarding the duniya) : In a study circle, there is a duniya part and an akhira part. What is the duniya part? Having the chairs, rugs, pillows, blankets, tables, food, etc. but what is the akhira part? The knowledge, the dealing with people, the good deeds, etc. What should you minimize and what should you maximize? What you learn today, not what you eat today, subhan Allah. Minimize the duniya and maximize the akhira - say alhamdulliah for the duniya you have. The study circle is spoiled when people come for duniya because the intention is spoiled and it affects everyone. People come for socializing, etc. - This spoils the intention.

Gentleness : when dealing with people, do not be harsh, why create a problem between us?

Hadith:

Aishah (may Allah be pleased with her) reported: The Messenger of Allah said: "Allah is Gentle and loves gentleness in all matters"). - Bukhari and Muslim

Even when you joke with others, you do not know how it may hurt and affect others. Some people will even stop acquiring knowledge because of people's harshness, subhan Allah. You do not want to close this door to others.

Don't say people will take advantage if I am gentle, let them. Your gentleness will actually help you learn: you want a peaceful environment.

Take your time : everything will come in its own time, do not rush, especially when it comes to people. Not everyone can reform at the same time. Even when you speak, take your time, don't say something you might regret. And take your time when you learn and when you question.

Verify the knowledge : if someone is telling you some hadith, you have to verify it. If someone is telling you something about someone, don't act until you verify it. This is especially true when sending messages, etc.

And if you have these manners, then it will purify the heart with the help of Allah.

Summary of Manners of a Knowledge Seeker

1. Seeking knowledge is worship

2.Follow the way of the righteous predecessors

3.Fear of Allah (the Most High) accompanying you all the time (

4. Watchful of Allah

5. Good Manners

6. Be content with what you have (with respect to the duniya)

7. Gentleness

8. Take your time

9. Verify knowledge

May Allah (the Most High) make this a truthful entry and a truthful exit.

Ameen.

May Allah (the Most High) increase our knowledge. Ameen.

• Guidance and faith need fuel and their fuel is knowledge, what kind of knowledge? The beneficial knowledge that will increase your faith of the unseen. We cannot see Allah, the Last Day, the Messengers, but we need knowledge.

• Knowledge is not for the brain, but for the heart to give it life. The life of your "heart" is what you believe, not what you see. The parable that Allah gives for beneficial knowledge is like water coming from above. It means that our knowledge has to come from above, it is divine untouched by human hands.

• When you start in knowledge, you feel excited about the information but as you get deeper into it, and it is a lifelong journey, then you see yourself as filled with sins and that is a mercy from Allah. This period is critical because people may give up at this point but don't stop. The more you discover your faults, the more you need to increase the dose of knowledge. Then you will have taqwa, then your heart is purified and you taste the pleasure of knowledge. Earlier seekers of knowledge were so dedicated that to eat they would dip their cookie in something hot to eat it faster, subhan Allah. A student of knowledge was on his deathbed and he heard a hadith and asked for his paper to write it down in his notes, subhan Allah.

▪ To acquire knowledge, it is not about having a plan and saying I will become a teacher, unlike the duniya when you get a degree and say I will be a teacher, doctor, etc. To acquire knowledge is worship and Allah (the Most High) will open for you.

▪ The responsibility you will have in acquiring knowledge is great. If you don't have the right foundation, then the knowledge can be against you and can be a poison to you and others.

▪ Messengers never asked to be messengers, likewise students of knowledge do not ask to be teachers, Allah gives them. Now there are desires to want titles to be called 'scholar', 'da'ee', etc. May Allah (the Most High) protect us. Ameen. And it is more dangerous to want 'religious' titles than duniya titles because the first to be thrown into hellfire are those who wanted to be called 'scholar' but not for the sake of Allah (the Most High).

▪ You will encounter problems from knowledge students and teachers because the basis is wrong. It's not about knowledge first, but it's good and right manners. We don't want to be a fitna to others.

JEWELRY FOR THE KNOWLEDGE SEEKER

▪ A seeker of knowledge means that you have to go to the knowledge, it will not come to you. And the more you go to seek it, the more it will be given to you.

ORNAMENT IN THE KNOWLEDGE SEEKER ITSELF

▪ (1) Seeking knowledge is worship : The scholars said that knowledge is a secret prayer in the heart, subhan Allah. The more you learn knowledge, the more it impacts your heart. Seeking knowledge is one of the greatest worships after duties, better than voluntary ones. Seeking knowledge is struggling for the cause of Allah (the Most High) because it is spreading Islam peacefully. There are many virtues in seeking knowledge, even the angels lower their wings out of respect for the seeker of knowledge. The angels, the fish, the ants, all do istighfar for the seeker of knowledge. When Allah (the Most High) wants good for a servant, He will make him understand the details of the deen. But our problem is ingratitude when we complain about the students, the teacher, the seats, and so on. And of course Allah will test you for your gratitude.

• Surah At Tawbah 122: (And it is not (proper) for the believers to go out to fight all together. From every troop of them, only a part should go out, so that (those who remain behind) may be instructed in (Islamic) religion, and that they may warn their people when they return to them, so that they may guard themselves (from evil).)

• The intention of knowledge is to remove ignorance from myself and others. But it is important not to seek revenge through knowledge, for example if a wife is angry with her husband, she will say a hadith to make him feel bad but Allah (the Most High) knows our intentions. It is dangerous to use the Quran and Sunnah for your desires.

• (2) Any worship needs ikhlas and itiba' (following the Sunnah).

• Ikhlas: Surah Al Bayyinah 5: (And they were not commanded but to worship Allaah, and worship none but Him Alone (refraining from ascribing copartnership to Him), and perform As-Salaat (Iqaamat-as-Salaat) and give the Zakaat: and that is the right religion). When you seek knowledge, your heart may turn to others besides Allah. Which is better, seeking knowledge for five hours or staying at home reading the Qur'aan, praying, fasting? Seeking knowledge because you are struggling more, and you are remembering Allah (the Most High) with others, needs dedication. With ikhlas and knowledge you will reach a high level but knowledge without ikhlas will be the lowest.

What can spoil the ikhlas?

▪ You love to be a well-known student : you like to be the center of attention and to be known among the students.

▪ Love being number one in the class : having that good reputation among others.

▪ Love for others to admire and aggrandize you : it is only a feeling in the heart.

▪ Love of receiving gifts/money: righteous predecessors used to refuse gifts from rulers because they feared they might affect their intention. Even in school, students should not give gifts to teachers. And this should be more so in the deen.

▪ Love being praised, getting titles.

▪ Attending class just to get rid of the scorn of others: for example, someone may not be able to attend, so people will ask why he/she didn't come and put pressure on the person, who may end up lying, etc. And not everyone has the same nature, some people are shy and find it hard to say so.

Hadith: (Abu Hurairah (may Allah be pleased with him) said: The Messenger of Allah (the Most High) said: "A person who acquires (religious) knowledge, which is (usually) acquired to earn Allah's Pleasure, (but he acquires it for the sole reason) of securing worldly comforts will not even smell the fragrance of Jannah on the Day of Resurrection) - Abu Dawud Book 18, Hadith 1620

We have to be careful because Allah (the Most High) looks at our hearts. Someone may be acquiring knowledge to get a certificate and someone may be acquiring knowledge to be praised, which is worse? Seeking it to be praised. Ikhlas is to seek praise and good reputation only from Allah (the Most High), not from others, not even from angels - we want nothing from slaves. We are poor and cannot see the whole picture. Allah (the Most High) is the One Who rewards and punishes and in His Hands is everything.

ORNAMENT OF BEING IN THE WAY OF COMPANIONS

They are those who preceded us in the faith of companions and followers (tabieen). Do not look at those who are currently with you because their 'exam' is not finished. You want to take the results of those who have already finished and passed. The way of the righteous predecessors is to learn without arguing. Their way was 'we listen, we believe and we obey'. Sometimes we argue just to prove our point of view, for our ego. Make knowledge easy for yourself, do not make it difficult. If you do not understand, Allah (the Most High) will make you understand when the time comes. What can you say after 'Allah (the Most High) says and the Prophet (peace and blessings of Allah be upon him) says'? Subhan Allah. Iblis was expelled from paradise because he argued with Allah (the Most High), he said 'he was created from clay and I from fire', subhan Allah. Religion by itself is beautiful and complete, you don't need to argue.

▪ The righteous predecessors did not go and bring things from their minds. Those who only philosophize have no proof, they just think and think and end up with a different belief, subhan Allah. For example, Allah (the Most High) says that He rose above the throne, but what do people who philosophize say?

How He rose above the throne, istaghfar Allah. And some cannot explain it so they deny it completely. We just have to believe, we cannot understand Allah (the Most High). This ends up leading to deviation.

THE ADORNMENT OF ALWAYS FEARING ALLAH

• To really benefit from knowledge, you need to always fear Allah. Just like a student in school is afraid of failure so he is motivated to do good. A seeker of knowledge fears Allah. Someone who does not fear Allah (the Most High) may learn, but there will be no barakah in his knowledge - he will not act upon it, he will do the opposite of knowledge, he will forget it and fail, thus losing the reward, may Allah (the Most High) protect us. Ameen.

• He who fears Allah (the Most High), then Allah (the Most High) will put barakah on his knowledge, increase him in guidance, faith and taqwa. He will act upon the knowledge without even realizing it, subhan Allah.

May Allah (the Most High) make us true seekers of knowledge. Ameen

• (1) Seeking knowledge is a worship

▪(2) Any worship needs ikhlas and itiba' (following the Sunnah).

(2) ORNAMENT OF BEING IN THE WAY OF COMPANIONS.

(3) THE COMMANDMENT TO ALWAYS FEAR ALLAH

(4) CONSTANT WATCHING

▪ Our eyes should be on our heart all the time because we know that Allah (the Most High) watches our heart. We have to watch our heart every moment for disregard, envy, enmity, etc. And when you fear Allah (the Most High) then the result is to constantly watch your heart → and this is actually ihsan which is to worship Allah (the Most High) as if you see Him.

▪ It is also important to watch our heart not to judge others, for example, you may see two people arguing, what do you feel inside your heart? Are you judging them? Or a student answers incorrectly, what do you think inside your heart?

(5) ORNAMENT OF "LOWERING THE WING" AND NOT BEING ARROGANT▪

Some people who have so much knowledge end up becoming arrogant and feeling better than others. This is just a feeling in the heart. Never think you are better than your husband, children, etc just because you are learning. You have to be humble, what's the use of learning if at home you talk bad about others? That is why it is important to have manners before knowledge.

▪ One of the scholars said that when he leaves home he feels that everyone is better than him, subhan Allah.

▪ The student of knowledge cannot be studying and looking at what others have of wealth, property, etc. For example, in school people may be looking at what is in their lunch box, what is in their stationery case.

Hadith:

It was narrated that Sahl bin Sa'd AsSa'idi said: "A man came to the Prophet (peace and blessings of Allah be upon him) and said: 'O Messenger of Allah, show me an action that, if I do it, Allah will love me and people will love me'. The Messenger of Allah (the Most High) said: 'Be indifferent towards this world and Allah will love you. Be indifferent towards that which is in the hands of the people, and they will love you."). - Ibn Majah Book 37, Hadith 4241

We do not like it when someone asks us for alms or a seller follows us to buy something. We should be lenient when people make mistakes, and everyone makes mistakes. Knowledge is so easily accessible but how can anyone carry the inheritance of the Prophet (peace and blessings of Allah be upon him) without having manners, subhan Allah.

(6) ORNAMENTATION OF THE BEST OF CHARACTER

• You need to smile at others, say salam, not be serious or frown. When you are in knowledge, you need to be easy and not harsh with others. This creates a welcoming environment, imagine everyone serious and frowning, this is unwelcoming. Unfortunately when people get into knowledge they become very serious with others but this is not the point. The study of deen is the best study because you are studying to heal the hearts to go to paradise, subhan Allah. The Prophet (peace and blessings of Allah be upon him) was very gentle, he never scolded anyone in front of others, he was easy going, how can anyone learn from someone who frowns and is afraid of him? Subhan Allah.

(7) ORNAMENT OF MEEKNESS

▪ You can't be harsh in your dealings with others, you need a gentle atmosphere with the people around you and with outsiders. You need to be gentle even in the way you place your belongings, when you give something to others, even your body language should reflect gentleness.

Hadith (Narrated `Aisha (Allah be pleased with her): A group of Jews asked permission to visit the Prophet (and when they were admitted) they said: "As-Samu 'Alaika (Death be upon you)". I said (to them), "But death and Allah's curse be upon you!". The Prophet (peace and blessings of Allah be upon him) said, "O `Aisha! Allah is kind and lenient and He likes one to be kind and lenient in all matters."). - Sahih al-Bukhari 6927

8) ADORNMENT OF VERIFYING▪ No hadith or dua'a or news can be taken without first verifying that it is authentic.

STAGES OF KNOWLEDGE

Ibn Al Qayyim may Allah have mercy on him said that there are six levels of knowledge.

1. Listening well : you are focused to listen well, even if you don't understand the language.

2. Ask well : this is the second stage that when you start the knowledge you ask to repeat things, what is this, etc, but it is important not to interrupt and only ask questions after class.

3. Understand well : e.g. you hear the concept and you understand it, now it clicks, e.g. you understand the concept of taqwa.

4. Memorize well : after listening and understanding, memorize.

5. Teach well : how can you teach others without having memorized the Qur'an and Sunnah? Subhan Allah.

6. Act upon it well : finally you can act after the previous stages.

• We have to see what level we are placed in or we are skipping levels.

(1) ORNAMENT WITH GREAT DETERMINATION

• When you seek knowledge, you need to have great concern and determination for it - you want to learn who Allah (the Most High) is, you want to study the Qur'an and Sunnah. Do not make the pursuit of knowledge just a pastime.

• Some have no facilities, sit on the floor, use chalk, sit in the heat, but why do they struggle? Because they have great determination and a great desire to learn. That's why it's important that we don't complain or be ungrateful for everything we have.

• When you are eager and determined for knowledge, you don't waste time. You won't let things affect you, for example an argument between you and another person, you won't put it in your heart, you won't let it distract you from learning. When you have a goal in front of you, you will not let pain affect you. Also when you have great determination, you will not humiliate others or compete with others because your focus is higher. Whoever seeks knowledge, then Allah (the Most High) will make the way to paradise easy for him.

(2) ORNAMENT WITH WANTING MORE IN SEEKING KNOWLEDGE▪

You're not satisfied and you want more. And there are two ways to nourish ourselves: the hard way or the easy way. Either with knowledge or by going through a difficult experience. We want to be nourished the easy way with knowledge, so knowledge is a great mercy to us.

May Allah (the Most High) keep His favors upon us and never deprive us. Ameen.

(3) ADORNMENT ON YOUR WAY TO THE PURSUIT OF KNOWLEDGE

▪ When you seek knowledge, you have to make the effort to go and seek it. And when you go, you will not only learn the curriculum itself, but you will learn in your interactions with others. There are people who just attend study circles even if they don't understand, but they want angels to surround them, mercy and tranquility to fall upon them. That is why no one is at loss when they attend study circles.

(4) ORNAMENT IN PRESERVING THE KNOWLEDGE WITH WRITING▪

Strive to take notes and alhamdullillah Allah (the Most High) made it easy for us to have recordings as well. Also don't depend only on someone else, you don't know who will read it and who it will reach. Even if no one reads the notes at least your notes will testify in your favor on the Day of Judgment, subhan Allah.

▪ Sometimes we hear something we really like and we say we will remember it and write it down later and then at the time of writing it down we forget it completely, subhan Allah.

▪ And people have different levels, some are good at writing, some at memorizing, and some at remembering,

And there is wisdom in all this that Allah (the Most High) gave us different talents.

(5) ADORNMENT IN SEEKING ALLAH'S HELP AND TRUSTING HIM▪

You need to trust Allah (the Most High) that He will help you and make acquiring knowledge easy for you - all these are just feelings in the heart. There is a grammar scholar who was told that at first he was weak in grammar so he was discouraged to continue until once he went outside and saw an ant going up and down, up and down, up and down, until the ant reached the top, so he decided to continue.

- Never give up on this journey even if you did not achieve or write because as long as you are a seeker of knowledge then Allah (the Most High) will reward you. Do not expect results because we feel good when we see results and get discouraged when we do not see them because it is not the results that matter but your actions of the heart - your tawakul, istiana'a, patience, etc. There will be messengers on the Day of Judgment who will have no followers, does this mean they are failures? No, but in our eyes we see it as failure. When we look at the results then the diseases of the heart appear - jealousy, comparison with others, etc.

- If Ibn Taymiyyah may Allah (the Most High) have mercy on him did not understand an ayah he would ask Allah (the Most High) to make him understand. He would say (O He Who taught Adam and Ibrahim, teach me, and He Who made Suleiman understand, make me understand). Ibn Taymiyyah brought this dua'a based on the Qur'an. So ask Allah to teach you and make you understand. Sometimes we ask someone to explain something to us and we are even more confused than before.

(6) ORNAMENT IN GIVING THE SOURCE

▪ It is important to mention the reference and source of all material.

(7) ORNAMENT IN BEING TRUTHFUL

▪ Do not say things about Allah and the Prophet (peace and blessings of Allah be upon him) that are not correct. And do not say that so-and-so said this if you are not sure. One of the scholars said that you have to learn truthfulness before seeking knowledge. You cannot be a student of knowledge and lie to others, istaghfar Allah.

▪ What leads a student of knowledge to lie? To prove his point or defend and it's all based on ego.

(8) ORNAMENT OF THE SHIELD OF STUDENT OF KNOWLEDGE▪

These are important words for the student of knowledge - 'I don't know'. It is OK to say you don't know, and scholars say that if you say 'I don't know' it is as if you have answered.

▪ Shaykh ibn Baz may Allah (the Most High) have mercy on him, who is one of the great scholars came to the conference and told his students that he did not prepare his lesson, although he does not need to prepare a lesson, but it is to show that it is okay if you do not know or did not do it.

▪ It also shows impoliteness when you complete the teacher's hadith or ayah because it is not about knowledge but about your behavior. One of the scholars was approached by a student who was excited to tell him a hadith. Although the scholar knew this hadith before the student was born, he allowed him to say it, and did not complete the hadith for him to prove that he knew it. This shows good manners.

▪ If someone asks you about a fatwa and you say 'I don't know' then you have already answered.

(9) ORNAMENT TO PROTECT YOUR CAPITAL: YOUR TIME

▪ We do not want to be wasting time, thinking about this or that, we want all our 24 hours to be rewarded, may Allah help us. Ameen.

(10) ORNAMENT IN RELAXING

▪ You can't be acquiring knowledge all the time, otherwise you will get tired, but when you do something else then it will help re-energize you to acquire knowledge again. If you like to cook, paint, spend time on yourself, etc. Even while doing something else you will be rewarded because you are doing it to revitalize yourself and go back to seeking knowledge.

▪ Your body has rights, your spouse has rights, your children have rights - you cannot neglect them, and when you take care of these rights then Allah (the Most High) will put barakah on your affairs.

(11) ORNAMENT IN THE REVISION

▪ Even if it's just 10 minutes to review or you can review with a friend.

(12) ORNAMENT IN REQUESTING GOOD

How to ask a question? First you have to listen well to the end and ask Allah (the Most High) to answer your question because it might be answered throughout the lecture. Trust Allah (the Most High) to get your answers. Sometimes you have a question and someone else asks the same question. You also need to ask Allah (the Most High) to understand it correctly.

• Sometimes you ask someone and you don't get the answer you like, so you go and ask someone else until you get the answer you like, and this causes fitna. Don't go to a teacher and say so and so teacher said this, this creates conflict and discomfort towards others.

• Or someone might ask a question just to challenge the teacher and Allah (the Most High) knows our intentions. That is why it is important to have the right behavior when asking questions. May Allah make us worthy to carry the inheritance of the Prophet (peace and blessings of Allah be upon him). Ameen.

• Islam is to teach us manners. May Allah (the Most High) give us the best manners. Ameen.

ORNAMENT OF APPLYING KNOWLEDGE

• Application comes with movements of the hearts first - being afraid, taqwa, etc. Note that after prayer we ask Allah (the Most High) for beneficial knowledge.

Signs of beneficial knowledge:

Beneficial knowledge is being applied : either you are applying it or you are in the process of applying it. It may be difficult, but at least you are trying.

Hating to be praised or elevated by people : this is a sign of beneficial knowledge that you hate when people praise you because you want your reward from Allah (the Most High). If someone praises you, you cannot be rude and tell the person not to praise you, but inside you hate it.

Flee from fame and duniya : do not ask for titles or positions, do not want to be known by others. As said before, Allah (the Most High) will give it to you without asking for it.

Stop claiming to be knowledgeable : don't say that you know or that you are a scholar or that you have a lot of knowledge.

Thinking badly of yourself and well of others : it is a sign that you have learned your lesson when you think badly of yourself and well of others. As you learn, you should be more humble. Even if people make mistakes, still think well of others. Ahmed bin

Hanbal said that if he sees someone with wine dripping from his beard, he will give the excuse that someone must have poured wine on his beard, and he will not say that he is drinking, subhan Allah. So if someone says something bad to you, just give him an excuse that he did not mean it. May Allah adorn us with all these jewels. Ameen.

MANNERS DURING THE LECTURE

▪ You have to have good manners because angels are present in the study circle. You have to have manners when sitting, when speaking, when dealing with others. Study circles are gardens of paradise, but how can they be gardens of paradise? When there are good manners. May Allah (the Most High) grant us good manners. Ameen.

STUDENT'S MANNERS WITH THE TEACHER

Respect the teacher : there should be boundaries and respect with the teacher, especially because he is teaching you the Quran and Sunnah. Sheikh bin Uthaymeen said that if you respect the teacher then that is the way of success for you.

Surah As Saff 5:

And (remember) when Mûsa (Moses) said to his people: "O my people, why do ye trouble me when ye know indeed that I am the Messenger of Allaah to you? And when they turned away (from the Path of Allaah), Allaah turned away their hearts (from the Straight Path). And Allaah does not guide the people who are Faasiqûn (the rebellious, the disobedient to Allaah). - Why did they not benefit from His messenger and their hearts went astray? Because they did not respect the messenger. It is important not to interrupt the teacher and not to insist because it may make the pupil proud and the teacher fed up. When a person disrespects the teacher, then he will be deprived of knowledge.

When the teacher makes a mistake : do not claim purity from anyone, do not say that this teacher never makes mistakes or never gets angry, you will see that the teacher will do the opposite because Allah wants to teach you that no one is perfect except Him. Why should we elevate anyone? The teacher is also human and can make mistakes. If you want Allah (the Most High) to overlook your mistakes, then overlook the mistakes of others. Some even defame their teachers, which is worse than defaming your friends, subhan Allah.

Don't get on the teacher's nerves : don't misbehave or challenge the teacher. Do not pressure the teacher to lose his or her temper.

Moving on to another teacher : when you feel that you have acquired all the knowledge, manners, etc. of the teacher and you want to move on to another higher level, you should not move on just like that, but you should say 'jazak Allah khair' to the teacher and tell him that you want to go to another place. You should also ask the teacher where you want to go. This will make the relationship between the teacher and the student healthier. You ask the teacher for permission to go and ask him where to go. When this happens, there are no bad feelings between anyone. Remember that in Surah Al Kahf, Al Khidr, who is the teacher, left the student, he left Musa ; Musa did not leave him. Keep in mind that you are learning for the sake of Allah (the Most High) and the important thing is to please Allah (the Most High) and go to paradise.

5. Take good manners and avoid imitating : what do we take from the teacher? Good manners that are based on the Quran and Sunnah. We cannot imitate and be like others. Some students love the teacher so much that they imitate him in the way he walks, talks, etc.

MANNERS WITH OTHER STUDENTS

There are three types of friends, you must make friends with one and leave the others:

1. Friends for benefits : you are friends with each other simply because you benefit each other for duniya, when you help them, they help you, etc. When there is no benefit, then they leave you, and the scholar called this person an enemy because they only want something from you otherwise they leave you. This shows impure friendship.

2. Friends for pleasure : you only enjoy their company, but there is no benefit from the deen or duniya. This type of friend is not eternal and is also an enemy because it is just a waste of your time.

3. Friends with virtues : with this friend they want everything to be a reward, this person will take you to paradise not others. The people of the duniya do not like this kind of people because they think of the hereafter. This friend will remind you of good, advise you, make dua'a for you in your absence. May Allah (the Most High) grant us righteous friends. Ameen.

Sincerity

Sincerity is that if a person does any good deed, he should do it for the sake of Allah.

To get reward from Allah and success in the Hereafter.

Do it for the religion, do it for good.

That act should be done keeping in mind Allah's Will, Allah's liking and he should do it for seeking reward from Allah.

He should not do it for seeking fame of this world, to get wealth and worldly things, to get some position or win the hearts of people in the world.

Whatever work he does, he should not do it for praise.

He should do it for the praise of Allah instead of the praise of creation.

Instead of getting the return from creation, he should seek the reward from Allah.

Instead of doing for this world, he should do it for the hereafter.

Especially, he should do the work of religion for the hereafter.

Allah has made sincerity obligatory.

In all deeds, all acts of worship, in all good deeds, sincerity is obligatory.

Allah, the Exalted, says

In Surah Al-Bayyinah, verse 5, Allah says:

They were only ordered for this thing

That they should worship Allah and make all of their worship sincerely and solely for Allah

Their whole religion, here religion means worship and action.

The whole of one's religion meaning the whole of his actions and the whole of his worship, one should be doing it sincerely for the sake of Allah alone.

The student of Knowledge should worship Allah by gaining knowledge with the intention of doing it only for Allah.

Sincerity is for the worship of Allah, to be done only for Allah.

Deeds legislated by Allah should be done only to please Allah.

Not for the praise of the creation or for any worldly gains.

So sincerity is obligatory, why?

Because it is known from this verse.

They were ordered to do so.

So from this verse it is known that sincerity has been commanded by Allah.

Allah's order was not only that they should worship Allah.

Rather. Allah's order was that: Worship Allah by submitting your whole religion for Allah sincerely.

So we come to know that worship alone is not enough.

Rather, sincere worship is desired.

Do not worship anyone other than Allah.

And worship of Allah should only be done for Allah alone, this is sincerity.

So from this verse, it is known that sincerity is obligatory.

And it has not been mentioned that in which act of worship sincerity is obligatory,

Rather, there is a generalization in it.

It has been generally stated that sincerity is obligatory in all acts of worship.

And it is obvious that knowledge is also one of the acts of worship.

Rather, knowledge is worship, since it has been ordered.

Seeking knowledge is also one of the acts of worship.

Rather, knowledge is a condition for all acts of worship to be correct.

If a person does not have knowledge, then no worship can be correct.

Rather, his belief cannot be right without knowledge.

Therefore, sincerity is also necessary in seeking knowledge.

This is the reason why the Prophet of Allah, peace be upon him, condemned those who seek knowledge for fame.

The Prophet of Allah (peace and blessings be upon him) said: Whoever acquires knowledge so he can argue with the people who have less understanding and put them into doubts and confusion

Or he seeks knowledge to compete with the scholars.

Wanting his name to appear in the list of scholars.

Wanting to be from the scholars and appear as one to the people.

Wanting to be in a position equal to the scholars.

Or turn people's faces towards himself.

Attracting people towards himself.

Expecting the praise of the people.

Such a person will go to hell.

This hadith has been narrated by Imam Ibn Majah.

This hadith shows that all three intentions are wrong.

A person becomes a speaker and a speaker that confuses people for no reason.

He is not a truthful speaker, rather he argues with the people.

He gains knowledge to overcome people of lesser understanding.

Argue and debate with them and confuse them.

If he acquires knowledge to prove his superiority above people, then such a person is in hell.

Or such a man who from knowledge he aims fame.

And people begin to consider him equivalent to scholars.

He wants the status and respect of scholars.

Such a person is also in hell.

Or get fame among the people who will say: Look, how much knowledge and wisdom this man has.

For this reason, he wants people to pay attention to him, people should start asking and watching him, people should become his followers.

If he is seeking knowledge for this reason that he wins their hearts by turning their faces towards himself, and make a place in their hearts.

If he is doing it for that reason then such a man is in hell.

It is known from this hadith that acquiring knowledge for the praise of people, gaining knowledge from worldly knowledge to attain higher position, or gaining knowledge to overcome people, all these intentions are bad intentions.

A student of knowledge should have good intentions.

If he wants to acquire knowledge, then his intention should be good.

What should be his intention?

It is the command of Allah.

Allah has made it obligatory.

Therefore, he should acquire knowledge by fulfilling the command of Allah.

Similarly, seek knowledge to remove oneself from ignorance.

Learn to lift others out of ignorance.

Similarly, seek knowledge to safeguard it.

Safeguard knowledge to spread it.

Arrows are coming towards the religion from its enemies and opponents.

The attacks on the religion that are taking place, people are making blasphemous statements about Allah, upon the Messenger, upon the Quran.

Seek knowledge to defend the religion from them.

Seek knowledge for rectifying the destruction that the people of innovation cause in the religion.

And similarly, the people of kufr and shirk who create doubts about Islam, and those who slander Allah and His Messenger

Seek knowledge to defend it against them.

If a person acquires knowledge with these intentions, it is a good intention.

He should seek knowledge to make the statement of Tawheed - the highest.

So that falsehood falls and the truth rises.

If he gets knowledge for these reasons, then he is getting knowledge rightly and his intention is good.

So the first thing we saw is that the student should have the right intention.

It is obvious that knowledge is in the heart of man.

And the intention is also in the heart of a man.

If the intention of a person is wrong, then after that whatever knowledge he seeks, it is very possible that it will harm him.

Unless, Allah saves him and bestows upon him the ability to be sincere.

Respect the Scholars

Another important thing for a student of knowledge to consider is the respect of the scholars.

Attending the service of the scholars and asking them politely.

Acquiring knowledge with respect.

Keeping their greatness in the heart and respecting their words.

And it is very important to follow Islamic manners in asking and learning.

Misbehaving with the scholars, making them suffer, making fun of them, to listen to their words with no interest and careless behavior, or to show your superiority in front of them by arguing with them for no reason, this is not from the manners of a student of knowledge.

Respecting the scholars is also religion.

This is what we find in the salaf as a norm.

The Messenger of Allah, peace be upon him, says:

He is not one among us who does not respect or honor our elders, and does not have mercy upon our young ones, and does not recognize the rights of our scholars

This hadith has been narrated by Imam Ahmad and Hakim.

In this hadith, if you think about it, there are scholars among the elders, but the scholars are mentioned separately because of their greatness, because of their special position.

It is clear from this hadith that the scholar has a right over the people.

The strange thing is that people think that they have a right over the scholar.

That is why you will see many people bothering the scholars.

And take services from the scholars.

They will ask questions by calling them at two or three o'clock in the night without thinking that it is time for them to rest.

If the people send the scholars a message but don't get a response, they get upset.

Then bitter messages will be sent that, 'you're doing such a thing even after being a scholar, that you do not answer our question and many such ridiculous things"

Rather, some people joke with the scholars.

They will stand with hands around their necks and so on and will assume that the scholars are growing up because of them.

And at times, some people wander in the company of scholars and try to make themselves appear bigger.

Not that they benefited from them.

So all these things are bad.

A scholar should be magnified and honored.

And we should acknowledge the right of the scholar over us.

To serve him, to support him in his religious cause.

To make things easy for him.

All these things should be for the scholar.

Rather, if someone criticizes him, then he should be defended.

If there is any suspicion about him, then his suspicion should be removed.

If someone is talking bad about him, he should be stopped.

Respect for scholars is respect for the knowledge of religion.

And respect for religion is salvation in terms of the hereafter.

If a man does not respect scholars, he will not respect knowledge.

And whoever does not respect knowledge is not respecting the religion.

He will be deprived of religion.

That is why one should not misrepresent any scholar.

Rather, if there is any mistake from a scholar, even then it should be overlooked.

Maybe that scholar will change himself and this man will be deprived of this scholar.

Even if a scholar makes a mistake, he knows the remedy for his mistake.

He also knows how to repay for the mistake.

And very likely due to his virtues Allah might forgive his mistakes.

May be because of his efforts in the religion and good deeds, Allah may forgive and overlook his mistakes.

This is very possible. If a woman gives water to a dog, Allah forgives her despite of her being a prostitute.

So the one who feeds the knowledge revealed by Allah to humans.

Such a scholar who is equipping them with the religion of Allah, why will such a scholar not be forgiven?

It is very possible that Allah may forgive him, considering that if not today or tomorrow, he will repent to Allah, he will repent for his mistake.

So here we should see that some people observe only a single thing of a scholar, then they insult the scholar in the whole world

This should not be the case.

The same people do not do this about their parents, while the scholar has more right than the parent.

The Prophet of Allah said that I am like a father to you, I teach you.

From this we come to know the position of teachers is like a father.

Therefore, a scholar should be respected.

Especially those scholars from whom we are getting knowledge.

They have a special right over us.

So from this hadith. it is clear that knowing the right of the scholar is also a blessing.

And if he does not know what is the right of the scholar over him, the Messenger of Allah, may God bless him and grant him peace, says he is not one of us.

He is not one of us does not mean that he is excluded from Islam.

He is not one of us means he is not on our way.

He is not like us, and he is not on our methodology.

So from this hadith, we came to know a very important thing, that scholars have a special position in the Ummah.

Ta'oos, a student of Ibn Abbas says:

It is from the sunnah that four people should be respected: a scholar, the elderly, the ruler of the Muslims, and a father should be respected.

Respecting these four people is a Sunnah.

That is, this is the way of the Prophet, may Allah bless him and grant him peace/

It's the way of the Salaf and has always been the way of the people of truth.

And it is that the Scholar, the elderly, the ruler of the Muslims, and similarly a father, they all should be respected

And observe that he put the scholar as number one.

Because all good comes through them.

Even the ruler is in need of scholars in the implementation of Sharia law.

And he consults them and listens to their opinion.

So it is very important to respect the scholar.

Shaabi says:

Zayd Ibn Saabit, may Allah be pleased with him, once led the funeral prayer.

A mule was brought before them, so that he may ride on it.

At that time, Abdullah Ibn Abbas, may Allah be pleased with him came to us/

And the place where the foot of the rider is placed - which is called Riqaab, he held it.

That is, he held it for him to keep his foot.

When Zayd Ibn Saabit, may Allah be pleased with him saw this he said, O Cousin of the Prophet, may God bless him and grant him peace, leave it, leave it.

- Ibn Abbas said "No". Rather, we honour our scholars and our elders this way.

This is how it has been done.

That is holding their riqaab, respecting them

We do this with the scholars.

We do this with our elderly

So imagine how the companions used to respect each other.

Zayd Ibn Sa'abit is a great companion.

The Sahabi who would to write the revelations of the Prophet of Allah, peace and blessings of Allah be upon him, so Ibn Abbas took hold of his riqaab.

The riqaab are held as a sign of respect.

So the thing is to respect the scholars.

To admire them has always been the norm of the salaf.

In the present era, the scholars have been made like one's average friend.

And people are joking with them.

Jesting with them.

Making fun of them.

And mocking them in their absence.

All these are the things of today which was not present at the time of the salaf.

Scholars should be mentioned with respect.

You can see for example that Ibn Abbas about whom the Prophet of Allah, may God bless him and grant him peace, himself has prayed. He especially prayed to Allah to grant him deep knowledge of religion.

What was their condition despite having so much knowledge?

He said: "I waited for a year to ask Umar bin Khattab. may God be pleased with him, about one verse."

Why did not he ask?

For a year I could not ask - Why I could not ask?

For the reason that his presence was so strong upon me that out of awe of him I was afraid to ask about a verse

Moreover that question was such that Umar ibn Khattab's own daughter was connected to the question.

The question was who were the wives upon whom Allah revealed a scolding to in the Quran?

So it was about his daughter

Ibn Abbas said he could not ask him out of his awe for him.

I waited for a year.

He said that once I was on a journey and was serving him the water for ablution, at that time I saw the opportunity and felt his mood. So seeing the opportunity, I asked at that time. So he said that they are Hafsa and Aisha about whom the verse was revealed which is in Surah At-Tahrim.

So you notice how the Sahaba used to respect the scholars.

The awe of scholars should be upon us, they should be respected.

So from this hadith, it is known from this tradition that sahabah used to respect great scholars, while they themself were knowledgeable.

But they still respected the scholars who were greater than them.

Respecting scholars, sitting in front of them politely, talking to them politely.

In today's era, this thing is disappearing, it should not happen.

So now, we know the second point that the student of knowledge should respect the scholars.

And there is a statement that is usually said amongst us: When a person respects the scholars, he honours them, so the knowledge that he takes from them has effect in his heart.

And as a result, glorification of the religion takes place in the heart.

But when he doesn't respect or honor the scholars, then the honor of knowledge will also have no effect in his heart, because it is coming from those very scholars (that he does not respect).

If they are not respected, then what will be the respect for their words?

When there is no respect for person, then what will be respect for his words?

But if he respects them, his words are also respected

And as a result, his religiosity increases.

So this is a very important point that the student of knowledge should pay heed to.

He should sit in the circles of knowledge politely and listen to knowledge with honor and glorification.

This is how it should happen.

Understand who are the scholars we have to have respect for.

When we say 'Scholars', it refers to those scholars who are Ahl al-Sunnah and not Ahl al-Bida'at.

Not those with corrupt methodology.

A person should acquire knowledge from these people.

He should acquire knowledge only from those sources which are reliable.

Scholars who are grounded in the Quran and Sunnah, who are upon the Manhaj of the Salaf and are pious.

Knowledge should be sought from such scholars.

The books of such scholars should be read - scholars who are trustworthy and reliable.

Do not read the book of such people who are not reliable.

No matter how famous they are.

Do not listen to the speeches of such people on YouTube or similarly elsewhere on the Internet

Do not listen to such people who are not credible.

Those who practice innovations.

And those who are not correct in their Manhaj.

Then there is also the matter of seeking knowledge from scholars that one should try more to seek knowledge from them directly (i.e., one to one)

Attend their gatherings and listen to them with your ears in their presence.

This was the method during the time of the Prophet of Allah, peace be upon him.

The Prophet said:

You will hear from me and those after you will hear from you.

And after you people will hear from those.

We come to know that knowledge comes from listening.

The method of seeking knowledge is that a person goes and sits in the circles of scholars.

And seek knowledge directly from them and listen to their words.

It will have special effect on the heart.

Later listenin to speeches on YouTube or on WhatsApp wherein an audio comes in, video clips come in, it has its own advantages but the right way of seeking knowledge is that a person should walk directly on his own.

Be present in such a gathering

And listen to the words of the scholars directly from their mouth.

Such a gathering has its own effect and has its own virtues.

Being surrounded by angels and in the same way the descent of tranquility.

And being praised by Allah.

Allah's mercy showering and covering such a gathering.

All these things are for religious gatherings.

So one should attend these circles.

It is known from this hadith that: You listen from me, people will listen from you and then those who have listened from you, people will listen from them."

This shows that knowledge is transferred from one group to another group

This shows that knowledge is transferred from one group to another group

And this is how we should gain knowledge.

It should not be the case that any man should suddenly stand up and start speaking.

And his followers increase.

So we see how many people follow him or how many people like his content.

Do not gain knowledge because they are famous or have skills in speaking.

Knowledge is not acquired for this reason.

Knowledge is acquired by seeing whom one has sought knowledge from.

How reliable is he? What do scholars have to say about him?

If we do not see things this way, then any and every man will be capable.

In terms of speaking, he will be an expert but he will be misguided.

And he will know how to turn the people's faces towards him.

And in such a case, we will go astray by listening to him.

So very important for a student of knowledge that they get knowledge from reliable sources.

Be it a speech or a book.

Get knowledge from people who are trustworthy.

Especially, they should give priority to the senior scholars in this.

Scholars who are experienced and have spent their lives in seeking and spreading knowledge.

Who have received thousands of questions and answered it.

Those who stay in research and have years of experience.

The words of such scholars should be preferred.

Especially when they have proof.

Abdullah Ibn Masood (may Allah be pleased with him) says:

You will always be on good terms as long as knowledge is in your elders.

You will always live well as long as knowledge is in your elders.

But when knowledge comes to your juniors, the juniors will start calling the seniors ignorant.

When we start taking knowledge from the juniors, they will grow big because of fame and they will forget their status.

And they will start speaking wrongly about the great scholars.

You see that today's era is similar.

So it is known from this tradition that as long as knowledge will continue to come from seniors, it will continue to come from above and goodness will remain.

When people will exempt the senior scholars and only seek junior scholars, if people start giving priority to junior's words, then a time will come that the senior scholars, whether they are of this era or of the previous era, less students of knowledge will gain knowledge from them.

So from this saying it is clear that one should get knowledge from seniors.

The sayings of the seniors should be referred to see what they have said.

Whether they are of our era or of the previous era.

The second thing is that it is important for the student not to acquire knowledge from the people of bid'ah.

Such people who are corrupted in the matters of aqeedah, manhaj or the sunnah.

Do not seek knowledge from such people.

Abu Umayah Al-Jumahi, a companion, says:

There are three signs among the signs of the day of Resurrection:

The Messenger of Allah (peace and blessings of Allah be upon him) said: There are three signs of the Hour.

Among these three signs, one sign is that knowledge will be acquired from the juniors.

Nu'aym Ibn Hammad says that Ibn Mubarak was asked who these juniors are.

One of the signs of the Resurrection is that knowledge will be taken from the juniors, so who are the juniors?

These are the people who speak their opinion.

Not on the basis of proofs, not on the basis of the texts of the Quran and Sunnah, but in matters of religion.

They make decisions based on their own opinions.

They speak based on what they think, based on desires.

But the junior who narrates from his seniors is not a junior.

Such a person is a student of knowledge but is connected to his seniors.

Lives under the guidance of the senior scholars above him.

He asks them and learns from them.

In big problems, he answers by taking their opinion.

And if people gain knowledge from such a student of knowledge, then there is no harm in it.

It's not bad neither its problematic.

The problem is with such a person does not have deep knowledge and not connected to anyone above.

He became self-confessed in his own way and started giving judgments to people with his own opinion.

Such a man is from the people of desires

One should not acquire knowledge from such a person.

This will increase when The Hour is near because people will not distinguish who is the senior and who is the junior.

People will just start looking at who is famous, who speaks well and then they will start learning from him and they will give wrong decisions and people will accept it.

Musa ibn Ayyub An'Naseebi says:

He said that Ibn Mubarak also used to say that the juniors, who are the juniors?

They are from the innovators, meaning the people of innovations.

So when the Day of Judgment is near, people will begin to gain knowledge from the people of bid'ah.

Clearly, near the Day of Judgment, people will listen and take knowledge from even the people of bidah.

Today you see how many people say that they like their speech.

They feel good because their words have an effect on the heart.

"The words of great scholars do not have the same effect on our hearts the way the words of so and so affects us, so we listen to them for it"

It will happen close to the Day of Judgment that people will take knowledge from people of bid'ah.

It has been described as a defect that even such a thing will happen close to the Day of Judgement.

So this is a terrible thing and should be avoided.

So the truth is taken from the people of knowledge, the people of truth.

That is why the famous saying of Ibn Sirin, may Allah have mercy on him,

This knowledge is your religion, so look from whom you are getting the knowledge from.

This shows that before acquiring knowledge it should be ascertained whether such a person is reliable or not.

The student of knowledge engages in knowledge that benefits

Engage in the knowledge that is most important and most beneficial to us.

The knowledge that is obligatory is more important. Do not engage in knowledge that is not useful.

Do not engage in such knowledge which is harmful.

And in the beginning, do not engage in knowledge which is not necessary to be sought in the first stage.

You must have seen many students who are students or have a passion for religion, they don't attain knowledge of the Quran and the Sunnah

But you'll see that they are reading the Bible, due to their passion for dawah, thinking they will give dawah to Christians.

Or they are reading the Vedas, thinking they will give dawah to Hindus.

While they do not know how to read the Quran properly.

While they do not even know the matters of ablution, how to pray.

Rather they don't even know the basics of belief

If asked about the proofs of Tawheed, they will not be able to say.

But tell us the evidence of Allah being Only One from Vedas.

Tell us from the Bible, then they will read it out, they will start reading verses from bible and the shlokas.

But the same issue, if we ask proof from Quran and Sunnah, they will not be able to give it.

It is a matter of great misfortune and a matter of deprivation.

Student of knowledge should engage in the knowledge that is really necessary and useful for him.

Abu Huraira (may Allah be pleased with him) said:

The Messenger of Allah (peace and blessings of Allah be upon him) used to supplicate:

O Allah, whatever knowledge You have given me,

Make it useful for me

Make it beneficial for me.

Whatever knowledge You have given me, give me the ability to benefit from it.

That is, to act upon it and to spread it.

And O Allah give me only that knowledge which is beneficial for me.

In it there is protection from knowledge which is not required and give me knowledge and increase in it.

This is a protection against having very little knowledge.

At times, a person tries to implement more but his knowledge is little.

He needs more knowledge.

Dua: Give me a lot of knowledge

There are three things in this Dua.

That he had that knowledge but he did not take benefit from it

He does not change himself neither he advises others

So this aspect is with which one begs Allah to make us among those who will benefit from Knowledge

Second one is he makes the mistake of engaging in knowledge which is not necessary for him or knowledge that is harmful for him

So it should also be avoided

O Allah give me such knowledge that is useful.

The third thing is that

He does not have as much knowledge as he needs.

The person knows few issues but he doesn't have knowledge for what he is responsible to do

So he said increase me in knowledge

Do not stop me in seeking or make me less knowledgeable, but make me more knowledgeable

It shows that the excess of knowledge is loved

A person needs to ask more knowledge from Allah

So here you will see

O Allah give me only that knowledge which is useful for me.

So a person should seek refuge with Allah from harmful knowledge.

That is why in a duaa in the hadith of the Prophet

The Prophet of Allah supplicated O Allah I seek your refuge from such knowledge that does not benefit."

And seek refuge from such knowledge which causes harm

That a man should learn magic to see what magicians do and what they do

Find out the knowledge of magic

Satan may try to tempt a person and

A person might do it and become a follower of disbelief or read the book of people of innovation.

What are the beliefs and methods in Sufism?

A person who is not grounded starts reading about them and may be misguided

Their doubts might enter his heart

or read the books of people of innovation to find out their arguments and proofs

He might start reading it while he is not firm upon his religion

He does not have the knowledge in depth and started looking at proofs of the people of innovation

There are chances he might get confused.

Or leaving the knowledge of Quran and Sunnah and started reading the Vedas and Bible.

Such a man will be at a loss and waste his time.

What he is responsible to, he did not get it.

How can one who does not know his religion become a da'ee of the religion?

One should not engage in knowledge that is either harmful or that knowledge which is meant for a later stage or that which he is not capable of

Many a times man doesn't know the basics of religion.

But goes deep into chains of narrations and narrators and so on

To see, how the hadith becomes weak delves into its intricacies

In many cases, he ends up becoming a Hadith Rejector due to stress he is unable to understand many things.

And he sees the differences of the scholars and starts disrespecting the status of the scholars.

So it is important that one focuses on obligatory knowledge in the first step.

So busy yourself in knowledge that benefits and not that which harms.

What is the foundation of the knowledge that benefits?

The knowledge that the Messenger taught the companions - the Quran and the Sunnah

Allah says

when Allah sent a Messenger among them who was from them

Allah sent from them, a human being, an arab, a Messenger

What does the Messenger do?

Recites the verses of Allah in their presence

And purifies them and reminds them.

He purifies them from wrong beliefs, bad habits and bad behavior

He teaches them the knowledge of the Book and wisdom

What is the knowledge that the messenger gives and teaches:

He teaches them the knowledge of the Book and wisdom

Although before that, their condition was that they were in complete misguidance

What knowledge was it to remove them from open misguidance that the messenger gave them?

It was the knowledge of The Book and Wisdom.

But what is the knowledge of the book and wisdom? This is verse 164 of Surah Al-Amran.

What is meant by The Book and wisdom? Ibn Kathir says

What is meant by the book and wisdom, is the Quran and the Sunnah,

He said this in Tafsir ibn Kathir. So we come to know

The Prophet used to teach the Quran and the Sunnah to the Companions

So we should acquire this knowledge if we want to save ourselves from misguidance.

That is why the Prophet of Allah, may Allah bless him and grant him peace, says

After me, I have left out two things in my speech if you hold these two things

You will not go astray after them.

That is. you cannot go astray after acting upon them

Those two things are the Book of Allah and my Sunnah.

So, to save yourself from misguidance, it is necessary to act upon the Book and the Sunnah.

Ikrama says

Ibn Abbas used to put shackles on my feet

And used to teach me the Quran and Sunnah.

Ikrima was the slave of Ibn Abbas

He said he used to chain my legs

He used to tie me and teach me, give me knowledge

Of what? The knowledge of the Quran and the Sunnah

We come to know that after the Prophet, may Allah bless him and grant him peace.

Later, the Sahaba also used to teach the Quran and Sunnah.

This is the useful knowledge that will give success, this is the foundation of all the sciences.

Those who are deprived of it are deprived of every good.

The knowledge of Quran and Sunnah is the foundation to which the student of knowledge should first turn.

So the fourth thing we have seen is that student of knowledge should prioritize beneficial knowledge.

And the knowledge of the Quran and the Sunnah, the acquisition of which is the most important

All the other sciences are either assistant of the Quran and Sunnah or either dependent on it. Remember this.

All the science, however many they may be. Whether it be to learn Arabic or to learn the principles of interpretation, the principles of hadith. And the principles of jurisprudence

Or in the same way, there is the knowledge of jurisprudence or any number of sciences

There is the knowledge of rijaal or the knowledge of Jarh wa l-ta dil or any number of sciences

They are either the assistants of the Quran and Sunnah

or they are the knowledge that are dependent and come from the Quran and Sunnah

So a student of knowledge should try to acquire these two sciences

And it should be prioritized over all because the foundational proof is the Quran and the Sunnah.

A student of knowledge should follow the Manhaj of the Salaf

He should respect the Salaf in his heart. He should practice the Manhaj of Salaf

Because even after acquiring the knowledge of the Quran and the Sunnah, if he does not have right Manhaj, he may take the wrong meaning from the Quran.

He may have take wrong meaning from the hadith.

It may be that he makes false statements that lead him astray.

That is why you will see in the past so many misguided sects who were present, none of them denied the Quran and Sunnah.

Rather, they argued in defense of their misguidance by quoting the Quran and the Sunnah as evidences.

They did not have the understanding of Salaf, that is why you will see that the Khawarij went astray on the basis of narrating the verse of the Quran.

They made their proof an ayah of the Quran

And by taking this verse, they declared Ali (Allah be pleased with him) to be a disbeliever. How did this misguidance originate?

Because of the application of this verse, they did not know how to apply it

When Ibn Abbas (may Allah be pleased with him) went to them

The first thing he said was Is there amongst you anyone in whose presence the Quran was revealed?

I came from those in whose presence the Quran was revealed.

So, if one doesn't have the manhaj of the salaf, then it is very possible that student of knowledge reads from here and there, gets the translation of the Quran, reads any explanation.

And then takes a hadith book and agrees with the translation

Learns the Quran word for word and gets a translation of a hadith book

And then start deriving meanings from them on his own.

If he does not have the knowledge of what the Salaf meant by it.

If he does not see this, he will be misguided.

Therefore, it is necessary to adopt the method of the Salaf while seeking knowledge.

The Prophet of Allah, peace be upon him, says:

Whoever among you lives after me will see many differences.

So it is necessary for you that you follow my Sunnah

And follow the Sunnah of the Caliphs Ar-Rashidun wal-Mahdi-in.

Mahdiin and Rashidin

Both Rushd and Hidayat are combined here in. Mahdiin and Rashidin.

The opposite of Hidayat (guidance) is misguidance and the opposite of Rushd is Ghivaya.

Misguidance is that a man goes on the wrong path due to lack of knowledge, this is misguidance

That's why the Christians are called misguided, because they were deprived of knowledge

They invented acts of worship and beliefs based on their opinion.

So misguidance means that if one goes wrong in knowledge without knowing.

Ghivayah is knowing the truth and then still follows the wrong path.

Both things were mentioned about the Caliphs

That they are not suffering from Ghiwayah or Dalala

On the other hand, it was said they were upon guidance.

They are on the right path with knowledge.

And they are Raashid.

Rather they are upon rushd which means while they are aware of guidance and they also follow it above their desires

Allah also said this about the Messenger

Allah combined the two things and negated them

What did Allah say?

Your companion - he is neither misguided, that is, he is not upon the wrong path without knowledge

nor is he on the wrong path out of desire

He speaks only out of revelation from Allah and acts upon only the revelation

It was said about the Caliphs that they are Mahdiin and they are Rashidin

Then the Prophet said: Hold firmly to it (meaning the Sunnah and the path of the Caliphs)

Hold it with your molar teeth firmly

And be wary and stay away from newly invented matters

Because every newly invented matter is an innovation and every innovation is misguidance.

Beware of the newly invented matters brought out in the religion.

There are many matters that have been brought together in this hadith

Number one of what was said here

Disagreement will come later and what should be done in such an era?

In the era of disagreement, whether it is religious disagreement or political disagreement,

The muslims should follow the Sunnah of the Prophet (peace and blessings of Allah be upon him)

and along with it, they should also follow the Sunnah of the rightly guided Caliphs.

The Prophet did not say only the Sunnah, but added the rightly guided Caliphs as well.

Also added the Salaf to it and then later said. Beware of innovation."

So we come to know that in the later period, due to differences, the people of innovation will be spread

Innovation will be everywhere. What should a Muslim do in such a period of disagreement?

During disagreement, not only the Book and the Sunnah to be followed, but along with it, its practical application, i.e., the manhaj of the salaf and how did they act upon it in terms of the aqeedah, we look at the salaf's understanding.

That is how they understood the beliefs.

And how did they act upon the rules of Allah.

This will save a person from going astray in terms of belief and action

From a narration we one to know further about this. Ibrahim At-Taymi says

One day, Umar bin Khattab, may Allah be pleased with him, was alone

So he was engrossed in a thought

He sent someone to call Ibn Abbas

When Ibn Abbas came, Umar ibn Khattab said, how will this Ummah fall into disagreement?

How can there be disagreement in this Ummah when its book is one, the Prophet is one and its qiblah is one, how can there be disagreement?"

He said, O Leader of the believers, the Quran was revealed among us, and we read it.

Read it and we know in what matter it was revealed.

We know which verse was revealed about what, and the Quran has been revealed infront us.

So we know on which occasion we should apply its verses.

But some people will come after us and will read the Quran

Without knowing which verse was revealed on which issue.

Which verse has come in which case.

Since they will not know which verse was revealed in which matter, everyone will have their own opinion.

When everyone has different opinions, they will have differences.

And when there will be a difference between them.

They will fight with each other and the differences will reach to the point of disagreements.

There will be disagreement because they will not know which verse was revealed concerning which issue

But who knew this? The Sahabah

For us, in order to avoid these conflicts, it is necessary that we turn to the Salaf

And this is also known from the hadith of the Prophet of Allah, peace and blessings of Allah be upon him.

That if there are differences later, then turn to my Sunnah and the Sunnah of the rightly guided Caliphs

So we come to know that some people will come after us and the text of the Quran will be in front of them.

But they will not be aware of its right application.

They will fit anything from anywhere and take any verse and start taking any meaning from it and will go astray.

It is strange that when the minds are different - one will understand this and other will understand that.

Then they will all fight amongst each other due to differences of opinion among themselves.

So, lack of understanding of the salaf is the cause of destruction.

Now let's see what is some advice of Imam Maalik for the student of knowledge.

Ibn Wahab relates from The Imam of Medina, Imam Malik ibn Anas, may Allah have mercy on him, that

He heard this from Imam Malik, that Imam Malik used to say

It is important for a person who is a student of knowledge to have dignity within himself

He should be calm, content and fearful of Allah, he should be dignified and not a gossiper.

There should be peace in him, he should not be rough handed, he who lives with dignity.

He should be one who talks and walks with tranquility and calmness while having the awe of Allah.

He should not be fearless or careless of Allah, Lord of the Worlds, he should not be careless of the hereafter.

Rather, he should fear Allah and the Hereafter, and there should be the awe of Allah within him.

And it is necessary that those scholars who passed before him.

Those who have gone before him should follow their footsteps.

So Imam Malik's advice for student is to have dignity, content and fear within one's personality.

He should be living with good manners and by fearing Allah

But it is also important that he follows the path of those who have passed away

Imam Malik had this special advice for the student that they should adopt the path of the Salaf

Do not be lazy and work hard.

Do not look for ease. Do not look for comfort where one is lying down and listening to a lecture on YouTube.

and he does not attend lectures, does not read books, and does not have any manners.

He does not want any difficulty but wants ease.

It is not appropriate. Knowledge needs one to strive for itself.

Walking to the gatherings of knowledge, sometimes in the sun, in the shade, in the cold, in the heat, in the rain.

Sitting for hours in gatherings and then reading books, researching and memorizing is hard work.

A man who wants knowledge to come to him by wishing is like standing on the shore of the sea and wanting for the sea to fall into his lap, it does not happen without working hard and running towards it.

Those who strive Our way, We guide them to Our ways.

If you want to get guidance from Allah, then you should strive for it.

Depending on the amount you strive is the amount of guidance one will receive.

This is verse 69 of Surah Al-Ankabut

In regards to this ayah, Shaykh Muhammad ibn Saleh ibn Uthaymeen, says the meaning of Jaahadu is

What does it mean to do mujahda?

In order to reach one's goal, he has put in a lot of hard work into it and said this is Jihad.

What really is Jihad? It is to work hard to reach your goal

To reach the goal, he has to bear hardships, go through difficult times, to fight. This is Jihad.

So the student of knowledge wishes that he gets knowledge, but it does not mean collecting books.

Some people keep collecting books and assume that knowledge has been gained, rather knowledge is what is in the heart.

Some of the salaf would even say that knowledge that cannot enter the bathroom along with me is not knowledge

That is, knowledge is what is in the chest, so collecting knowledge in the chest is the real knowledge.

So to acquire knowledge, whether it is memorization of texts or the understanding of those texts, both of them should be in the chest of men.

Knowledge does not come without striving.

In this relation let's see how much the salaf used to strive.

It is said regarding Jabir ibn Abdullah

He came to know about a hadith that a certain companion has this hadith.

He said. When I came to know that so-and-so Sahabi had a hadith.

Then I bought a camel and I tied onto it whatever is required for a journey.

And after traveling for a month, I went to Syria.

In another narration, Egypt is mentioned. So I traveled for a month and went to him.

When I reached there.

I saw Abdullah ibn Unais, who was a Companion, he was in Syria or Egypt,

I sent a man to go and say:

Jaabir is standing at the door."

The one whom he sent came back and asked Is it Jaabir ibn Abdullah?"

I said Yes, I am Jabir Ibn Abdullah."

Because there are many called Jaabir. so Jaabir, Jabir Ibn Abdullah?

So he said yes, that when he heard the name of Jabir Ibn Abdullah then Abdullah ibn Unais came out and hugged me.

Jaabir Ibn Abdullah said I got to know that you know a hadith which has not reached me.

I feared that death would come to me or to you before I could hear this hadith

that I might die or you might die so I have come to you.

He said the hadith which I heard from Prophet (peace and blessings of Allah be upon him)

Is that the people will be gathered on the Day of Judgement

unclothed and uncircumcised

Jaabir ibn Abdullah asked "What is buhmun? (which occurs in this Hadeeth)".

He said that they will not have anything, money, rupees, nothing then on the Day of Resurrection they will be raised with no clothes and without circumcision and they will not have any wealth or possession

Jabir ibn Abdullah traveled for a month to Abdullah ibn Unais for one hadith as it is mentioned in this narration.

So we see that he is a Sahabi who is so great and that Sahabi bought a camel especially for this one hadith.

Packed what is required to travel for a month and reached him only to ask about the hadith and he returned.

So this striving to seek knowledge is really great.

Today we are not able to attend lessons even in the nearby mosque.

So who is this student who wants to sit at home and listen to live lectures.

Although its possible to walk and being in the class. So all benefits which he needs to get will go away.

And you heard the verse.

We come to know that as much as a person strives for the sake of his religion,

Allah gives him as much of the guidance that he strives for.

It is a great blessing to receive guidance.

Sometimes knowledge is received but guidance is not obtained.

Hard work and striving are necessary for guidance.

The guidance which we ask in Surah Fatiha in every rakat.

Allah gives us that guidance upon striving so we should also try to strive.

The student should not seek rest.

He is memorizing Mutoon or Quran or Hadith.

He is memorizing proofs or memorizing the sayings of scholars.

There are texts or compositions of books that he is memorizing.

These are their books of knowledge.

So he should strive for these things. Likewise, if a person is sitting in a class.

Day-to-day lessons. For hours, he is sitting and struggling.

His back is aching, is tired and came from work.

One does not really succeed in the world without struggling.

Even if it is a matter of the worldly affairs, one has to work hard for it.

So for that if a man wants to get knowledge,

The student should be ready for striving.

It should not be case that knowledge or degree has been obtained, and now he sleeps in peace.

No. knowledge is a responsibility. When he has acquired knowledge.

After the permission of scholars, he should start spreading knowledge.

If it is a matter of independent lectures and talks, then permission should be taken from the scholars of whether he is really worthy of it or not.

And if generalization is to be done on an individual level, then it is permissible for him.

Propagate from me even if it is one verse.

Or as the Prophet said:

"May Allah keep such a person fresh and active

Who listens to a hadith from us and passes it on to others as it

Keeps it safe then delivers it."

Because many who deliver fiqh and ahadeeth are not jurisprudents themselves.

And many wisdom bearers convey to people who have more understanding of jurisprudence than them.

This hadith shows that it is not necessary to be a jurist for preaching

That is why Prophet (peace and blessings be upon him) said

That many hadith carriers,

Those who take the matter are not jurists themselves.

So, it is not necessary to be a scholar for what you want to preach.

Yes, if a person is announcing a lecture,

He is going on the stage and inviting the people,

And answering questions.

And explaining and interpreting the Hadith, the Quran.

It is important for him to have deep knowledge.

And for that, it is necessary that he asks the scholars above him whether he is worthy or not.

So it happens in every field of the world, so why not in the field of religion?

So the difference between the two should be remembered. There is no such issue in preaching.

A man can preach by knowing about even small matters.

But for a man to be a reference for people in the dawah field, it is necessary that he gets knowledge with depth and enters this field after the permission of scholars.

It is important to remember the difference between the above two.

Sulaym ibn Aamir says

We use to sit with the Companion of the Prophet (peace and blessing be upon him), Abu Imama al-Bahili

That is, we used to get the knowledge of religion by sitting with him.

So he used to tell us many ahadeeth of Allah's Messenger (may peace be upon him).

When he would stop after narrating his hadith,

When there would be a break in the gathering,

Do you remember this? Do you understand this?

As the word has reached you, now you convey it to others on our behalf.

As it was delivered to you, we delivered it to you, now you deliver it to others.

We come to know that the Companions used to narrate ahadith in front of the people.

And they would say to their disciples that now you also spread it.

This is how a student of knowledge should be.

He should take knowledge from the scholars and not hide it with himself.

Rather, make it known to people.

Knowledge is there to be spread.

So the knowledge taken from the scholars should be spread among the people.

Similarly Ibn al-Qasim, may Allah have mercy on him, says

When we use to part with Imam Malik,

Whether he goes on a trip or we go on a trip.

This is what Imam Malik used to say while parting with us.

What did Imam Malik advice?

This is the basic advice that is given to the student of knowledge.

And every human being is in need of it.

And that is fear Allah. If there is no fear of Allah, then everything will be harmful.

If a person does not fear Allah, then he will not be careful about the religion.

He might give any fatwas and may also mislead the people.

He can make Halal as Haraam and vice versa.

He can say wrong for what is right and vice versa.

Fear Allah, and spread this knowledge among the people.

Spread this Knowledge among the people.

Teach people and do not hide this knowledge.

Imam Malik used to say this to his students.

So it is clear from this that the salaf used to instruct the people to spread knowledge.

But here one point must also be remembered.

That every knowledge is not for every man. Because there are levels of knowledge.

Some knowledge are deep and difficult to understand.

And if a person falls into these things before it is time, then such a person can be a victim of horror.

Rather, he can be misguided.

He might start rejecting them.

Because if one does not understand something, he becomes its enemy and rejects it.

Ali (may Allah be pleased with him) says

Explain to people only those things that they can understand.

Do you like that people will deny Allah and His Messenger?

That is, explain only those things in front of the people what they can digest and understand.

If you will explain things in front of them which is above their understanding,

It is very possible that they will not understand,

Then they will deny it.

Only those things should be explained in front of the people which are appropriate in terms of level of understanding.

In the same way, Abdullah Ibn Masud, may Allah be pleased with him, said

Whenever you state something like that in front of people where their level of understanding does not reach

Their aqal (intellect) does not reach to that extent

If you tell them things above their understanding.

Those things will become a trial for some of them.

It will throw them into confusion and misguidance.

Sometimes something is right but the listener does not deserve to understand it.

Now his capacity to understand is not so much.

Without understanding, if we pour all those things in front of him.

He may start to doubt and start denying it.

So this is the trial that leads to denial.

It is forbidden to narrate everything one hears in front of people.

He has mentioned it in this chapter.

So remember to spread knowledge.

But look at the ranks of the people.

And see the level of understanding of every human being.

Explain it to them accordingly.

Sometimes a student studies a lot himself about the differences between scholars and the misguided sects.

And then starts to explain in front of every man.

So sometimes you are refuting someone but the listener takes this thing and views it to be correct.

Do not explain to him what is not necessary.

Explain to him that which he is capable to understand and that which he needs.

Do not spill on everyone all the information you have.

Rather a person should make a wise choice in sharing information.

Who needs what?

As a doctor does not give all medicines to all patients.

He gives the specific medicine to the specific patient who needs it.

It is the beauty of choice that makes him a good doctor.

So the diagnosis of individuals or the diagnosis of their diseases and its proper treatment - one should know this matter well: Who should be given what.

Avoid talking about the religion without knowledge.

A student should have a passion for spreading knowledge in his heart.

At the same time, in his heart he should be afraid not to say anything in the religion of Allah without knowledge.

He should keep his tongue in check.

And no matter should be spoken about without knowledge, without proof or without certainty.

He should not speak until he is firmly certain.

Allah says in the Quran

Surah Bani-Israel, Verse 36

Allah says

Don't pursue that which you have no knowledge of

For certainly the ears, eyes and heart

All of these things will be questioned.

Therefore, a person should be cautious about knowledge.

In the tafsir here, Ibn Abbas says

Do not speak without knowledge.

That one should not speak without knowledge.

That is why man will be caught on the Day of Judgment if he has spoken without knowledge.

Look at the Prophet (peace and blessings of Allah be upon him) himself

Jubayr Ibn Muta'im says

(who is a companion)

A man asked the Prophet of Allah, peace be upon him,

O Messenger of Allah, which of all places is the most loved by Allah?

The Messenger of Allah, peace and blessings be upon him. said:

"I can not tell until I ask Jibreel."

So Jibreel came and the Prophet asked him.

So he said that the places that Allah likes the most are the masajid.

And the most hated places in the sight of Allah are the markets.

Even though the Prophet of Allah, may God bless him and grant him peace, had such a high position.

When it was asked to the Prophet about something which he did not know, then the Prophet said I don't know.

A student should not be ashamed to say I don't know.

Indeed, one of the works of praise is that a person is famous, might be famous for knowledge, and if asked, he says I don't know.

A person cannot say this if he has no confidence.

Look at the case of Imam Maalik

A man from the people of the West came to Imam Maalik

And regarding a problem he asked.

Imam Malik replied I do not know.

The man said O Abu Abdullah, you say that you don't know.

That is, you are such a great scholar.

You have so much knowledge, you are the Imam of Madinah.

And a person such as you is saying I do not know?"

Imam Malik said. Yes,

Go to those people who sent you and tell them that I said I do not know."

That is, this courage is the result of having taqwa of Allah.

When a person fears Allah.

So he does not speak in religion without knowledge.

And he becomes so courageous that he says I don't know.

Along with knowledge, the student should also engage in worship and action.

Sometimes student considers knowledge as the real worship

And knowledge is considered special.

After gaining knowledge, he understands that I have become religious.

A man is not religious unless knowledge is practiced.

And knowledge in essence is not the ultimate goal.

The requirements of knowledge must be met.

Whether it is a matter of faith,

Whether it is a matter of worship or a matter of morals.

The requirement of knowledge is that a person should believe accordingly.

Speak accordingly and act accordingly.

Knowing alone is not salvation.

Rather, knowledge will become a proof against him on the Day of Resurrection.

If he has not acted upon it.

Therefore, the student should practice along with acquiring knowledge.

Allah says in the Quran

What is the situation that you command people to do good?

And forget yourself.

While you read the Book of Allah

Do you not have a mind?

We come to know that the person who has knowledge of the Book of Allah,

Advises people to do good

But does not practice goodness himself.

Such a man is neither knowledgeable nor does he have any intelligence

How can that man be intelligent who tries to save all the people but perishes himself.

Throws himself into destruction.

Invites all the people to run towards jannah.

And he runs towards hell.

Such a man cannot be intelligent.

We come to know that the student of knowledge should not forget himself.

Worrying about people and not worrying about himself.

He is not a true daee.

He is not scholar, he is not knowledgeable, he is not a student of knowledge.

The Prophet of Allah, may Allah bless him and grant him peace, says:

The steps of the son of Adam cannot be moved

He cannot turn away from the presence of Allah, from answering Allah

He cannot depart from his Lord on the Day of Judgment.

Until five questions are asked to him.

Until he is asked about five things

About his age.

What did he spend his life doing?

Where did he spend his youth?

And where did he earn his wealth from

And where did he spend his wealth

And from whatever he knew, what did he act upon?

It shows that on the Day of Resurrection.

Out of five questions, one question will be

How much of the knowledge that he knew did he act upon?

We all have to answer that.

So the student also has to prepare the answer by practicing it and by acting according to what one knows.

Sufyan At-Thawri says

Knowledge calls upon action.

If the call is answered through action, then its good. Otherwise the knowledge will fade away.

As someone comes to someone's door.

Gives a knock, gives a voice.

If no one responds from home, he goes back.

In the same way knowledge calls out to action.

If the call of knowledge is acted upon, then the knowledge remains.

Otherwise knowledge goes away.

His knowledge is lost.

Knowledge departs from him.

Likewise it is necessary for a student that knowledge should not be limited to information.

Rather, fill your heart with the remembrance of Allah.

Because knowledge and remembrance go hand in hand.

The knowledge without remembering Allah becomes information.

It doesn't create any value to a human being.

But the one who remembers Allah gets the right benefit from his knowledge.

Why? Because the remembrance of Allah creates fear in his heart.

It creates piety.

Allah's Prophet (peace and blessings of Allah be upon him) has described remembrance before knowledge here.

To know its importance.

Beware! The world is cursed

It leads to a curse

It will take you away from Allah's mercy

All that is in it is accursed

That is, it removes one from the mercy of Allah

Yes, but remembrance of Allah

The mention of Allah or that which is close to the remembrance.

When the remembrance of Allah comes to the heart, worship and commandments also come in life.

And except for remembrance and that which is closer to remembrance and scholars and students.

All of them are away from being cursed.

What was mentioned before the scholar and the student?

The remembrance of Allah and that which is related to the remembrance of Allah.

something connected with the remembrance of Allah.

So they are saved from being cursed.

So we come to know that along with knowledge, there should be also the remembrance of Allah in the heart.

The adhkaar after waking up in the morning.

Before sleeping, before eating and after eating,

When leaving the house, likewise dua of travelling,

Or in the same way, going to the masjid, going out, washroom etc.

As many adhkaar there are,

When the student practices them.

So his knowledge remains.

Moreover, he is connected to Allah in every situation.

Being connected to Allah makes him a practitioner of knowledge.

And saves him from carelessness in the matter of knowledge.

Hasan Al-Basri says

Acquire knowledge in such a way that worship is not harmed.

And engage in worship in such a way that knowledge is not harmed.

This is a lovely statement that should be remembered.

The student at times gets so busy in seeking knowledge that he loses his acts of worship

And sometimes people get so busy in worship, and it takes them away from knowledge.

A person should accumulate both knowledge and worship.

So the student should perform their acts of worship.

Do the sunnah, pray qiyaam and do the adhkaar

Make duaa, recite the Quran

In the same way, observe fasts to cut off your desire

In this way, do as many good deeds as there are

So worship should also be in the student's life.

Student of knowledge should purify his heart from diseases

Knowledge creates pride in a person just like wealth.

On the other hand, the wealthy do not have the same pride as the knowledgeable.

Because many wealthy people are also in need of knowledgeable people

They are honored and respected.

So knowledge has its own glory,

And the person who gets knowledge also becomes like a king.

And it creates pride in him.

People honor him, respect him and serve him.

His name is taken with respect and gestures are made towards him.

He starts thinking of himself as something superior.

Student of knowledge should avoid this disease.

He should not think himself to be superior.

He should always focus on his own shortcomings.

So that pride and arrogance do not arise in his heart.

Every human being no matter how good he is,

He cannot fulfill the right of worshiping Allah.

There will be some shortcoming in him.

The Prophet of Allah, peace and blessings of Allah be upon him,

For a while, if he the Prophet went to bathroom.

He used to come out and say Guf-raanak.

The scholars said in this explanation that the Prophet of Allah, may Allah bless him and grant him peace,

Being absent from remembrance even for such a short time, would regard it as negligence.

And asks Allah for forgiveness for that.

So this should be the attitude of a student of knowledge.

That even after doing everything and getting everything, I did nothing.

When the help of Allah comes and you see the victory.

And when you see that people are entering the religion of Allah in large numbers.

People are becoming Muslims by accepting your invitation.

So what should you do at this time? Show pride?

You should praise Allah and seek forgiveness from Allah.

Certainly Allah accepts repentance and forgives those who repent.

Tasbeeh, Tahmeed and Istighfaar!

Tasbih is describing the purity of Allah.

I am not pure, my work is not perfect, rather my work has shortcomings.

Allah is free from every shortcoming and I am the one with shortcomings.

Praise be to Allah, all praises are due to Allah.

I have done great things, but praise should not be mine.

If it were not for Allah's grace, I would not be able to do anything.

If Allah did not facilitate it for me, I would not be able to do anything.

Praise be to Allah, He made everything easy.

He is the one who gave the ability, he is the one who did everything.

And what is for me?

I have to repent.

Yes, I did but with the guidance of Allah, although there is also thanks and praise to Allah.

But there is repentance as well that I did not do as it should be done.

So these things, in the time of success, in the time of dominance.

The Prophet of Allah, may God bless him and grant him peace, is being advised.

The student should also be the same.

It is not that much religious work is being done through me.

And I have gained so much knowledge and I teach people so much.

And I have so many followers.

A man should not have pride in it.

Rather, a man should always keep an eye on his shortcomings.

There should be humility in the student of knowledge.

If there is no humility but rather there is arrogance, then he will be veiled from knowledge.

Arrogance becomes a veil between knowledge and him.

Indeed, a person who is arrogant cannot be guided by knowledge.

Allah says,

That soon We will deprive these people of Our signs with Our verses.

We will turn them away, those who are unjustly arrogant upon the earth.

Their condition is such that

They say no matter how many signs they see

They will not be blessed with faith.

No matter how many miracles or ayat of Allah they see in the sky and earth.

They are not given the grace of faith.

And even if they see the path of guidance, they still do not get the grace to follow it.

Who are those people?

Those who are unjustly arrogant and have pride upon the earth.

And this arrogance,

It becomes an obstacle in the understanding of the truth in one's faith.

Therefore, the student should never be from those who have pride.

This is verse 146 of Surah Al-Araf.

There is a hadith of the Prophet in this matter - Abdullah ibn Masood says

Allah's Messenger said

That person will never enter heaven, whose heart has even an ounce of pride.

Or self-praise.

A man said O Messenger of Allah a man likes that his clothes are good, his shoes are good.

So a man likes to wear good clothes so is this also considered pride?

He (peace and blessings of Allah be upon him) said that Allah is Beautiful.

But what is pride?

Exaggeration and arrogance is a man's denial of truth.

Rejecting the truth and treating people as inferior.

Contempt towards people, considering people as humiliated.

If there is such a man, then he is prideful.

And this was the pride of Satan, by denying Allah's Order.

Satan said Adam (peace be upon him) is lower than him.

So these two evils were present in Satan.

So Allah said: He refused and became prideful. He was one of the disbelievers.

So, arrogance is that a person thinks other people are lower than him and denies the truth.

If someone has knowledge and if one with lesser knowledge than him says something in front of him.

Or he explains his mistake, he does not accept it and thinks him to be lower than himself.

And he thinks low of people around him.

I have much knowledge while they have nothing.

They need me, they are ignorant.

They won't know until I tell them.

It is not a good thing to have this pride, such a person will not go to jannah.

The Prophet of Allah says

3 things will destroy

Desire, whom one starts indulging in, starts following it.

Greed to which one becomes a slave to.

and that he begins to think about himself as something big.

When a man starts to think that he is also something big, then he is destroyed.

So we come to know that if a person thinks something (big) of himself, then such a person perishes.

The Prophet of Allah found salvation in humility.

Think less of yourself.

Even after getting everything, I should realize that I was not really worthy of it.

It is Allah's grace and mercy that Allah has granted this opportunity.

So Allah's messenger says

Whichever slave practices humility for the sake of Allah, Allah raises him high.

A person who humbles for the sake of Allah, not for showing off, not faking his humility.

But really, in his heart,

He considers himself to be inferior.

And a person who keeps an eye on his shortcomings.

Considers himself inferior to others.

Allah raises him high.

Allah blesses him with blessings and raises him high in status and ranks.

Therefore, in the world too, we see a man who has pride, people hate him.

One who is humble, people love him.

Why? Because Allah puts love in the hearts of the people for him.

Whomever Allah loves. He also gives them the love of people.

So these were ten points that a student should remember.

There are many other points besides this as well.

But these ten things are essential if we do it.

Let's move forward by understanding and respecting things.

Other things can also become easy for us.

And these are things of very high priority.

So we pray to Allah, the Lord of the worlds, that He graces us to become good students of knowledge.

One who acquires beneficial knowledge, one who remains attached to the people of knowledge.

The one who spreads the knowledge of the religion and he who does not boast about himself.

But instead make us from those who seek and spread knowledge with humility.

And in the same way, the attributes that are required for knowledge.

One should be consistent in seeking knowledge and not back out from it. May Allah make us among those people.

May Allah accept our efforts and protect us from misguidance.

Reference: This book is based on the book of Shaykh bin Uthaymeen may Allah (the Most High) have mercy on him. A person took notes from the lecture and this book is based on those notes. Also this book is based on the lecture of Shaykh Abu Zaid Zameer in Urdu regarding this topic.

May Allah (the Most High) make us true seekers of knowledge and may he make us us mubarakeen. Ameen